THE BEAT
Life on the Streets

To Captain Michael Louis Fine (Lepcha),
great father, son, partner,
decorated US war veteran, superb pilot,
and wonderful brother

THE BEAT
Life on the Streets

DAVID FINE

SITRIC BOOKS

First published 2000 by
SITRIC BOOKS LTD
62-63 Sitric Road, Arbour Hill,
Dublin 7, Ireland.

1 3 5 7 9 10 8 6 4 2

A CIP record for this
title is available from
The British Library.

ISBN 1 903305 00 4

*All names of persons referred to
herein have been changed.*

Set in Sabon by Sheila Stephenson
Printed in Ireland by ßetaprint of Dublin

CONTENTS

ACKNOWLEDGMENTS

Joni Big Ears; Mad Man Langan and his Mot; Evil C; Goldie; Grawnz; Blunsky and Eilie; the godson and little-hand-on-my-face girl; Tash and her lunatic mother; Hannah and Janie Chrispin; Donkers; Loobie, Beeve and Harryzac; Gilbert and Walsh; Ann-Marie; Knarf and Peig; the Lark and his tall mate; Jim and his team; Professor Heather Höpfl; the conduits of the Running Deer (truly more grateful than you will ever know); Rashid; Michèle and the Yitzcocks; Carlow Girl and the bearded doctor; Swampy Snoyle; Howard Popeck of London; the girls downstairs; Pat the Tapper; Ashey; Fyodil Flappers; the lovely Susan and Sexy Babs; Vera 1 & 2; Mary 1 & 2; Karate Girl; Hilary; Patricia with the scanner; Donal from Cloyne; the nurses and doctors of Cherry Orchard Hospital; Mr Olima and Dr Nwosu; the gay couple down in the country;

Cousin Judith; Jason and Tina; The Mullet; Wishy and
Mary 3; Simon and Susan 2; Aherina; Serene Girl; May-
May (whose friendship will never die); the Auld Women of
Baggot Street; the Rabbi, whose ineptitude taught me a
lesson in life; and Blondie, for whom I had to fight (true
love never dies).

A very special thank you to Antony, Varese and Helen.
More special thanks to Ray Ebbs, a true friend who protected me from danger. Above all, he trusted and believed in
me. To Abba and Eema, who saved me from the abyss.

There are many more.

THE BEAT
Life on the Streets

PROLOGUE

THESE ARE TRUE STORIES from the Dublin underworld, recorded and written over two years as a taxi-driver. The girls are my friends. I have often driven around the area and lusted after some of them, but that is usually where it stops. I have twice tried to do business with the girls and had my offer of payment rejected (the second time with a very hard slap). I have loved them deeply, cuddled them, stroked their hair, and had them sleep with me all night. I have washed and dressed them when they were so sick that they couldn't do it themselves. I have been angry with them, but I have never judged them. What follows is an honest account of those experiences. All names have been changed.

I

'MISADVENTURE'

ONCE, I WAS *a nice Jewish boy from leafy middle-class Dublin, full of predictable ideals about love, marriage, education, a good job, keeping kosher and so on. I helped local Jewish charities and spent time in Israel. I aspired to having a pretty Jewish wife, plenty of money, and a position in the Orthodox community.*

But I was never really accepted, any more than my family was. We were hybrids: my mother had converted to Orthodoxy from Christianity (Methodism). She had embraced a religion and way of life known for being unwelcoming to converts. My father's Jewishness did not save the family's reputation. My two brothers and I weathered gibes and comments, fighting the internal bigotries that have always afflicted Ireland's Orthodox Jews. Later on we sought comfort and genuine welcome in the liberal Jewish community, where our Jewishness was confirmed and embraced.

I still aspired to basic Jewish values. I wanted to continue living as a practising Jew. I felt I needed a Jewish partner. When I couldn't find a nice Jewish wife in Dublin, I had to go farther afield.

When I went to Manchester in 1986, aged twenty-eight, I was the new boy on the block. It was great fun, and the many invitations I received and dates I went on massaged my shaky ego. I was confident of finding happiness. Eventually I married a religious Jewish girl and we set up house together.

But things went wrong from the start. To my wife's parents, I was a half-breed with no professional qualifications who had seduced their sweet, innocent daughter. They refused to have anything to do with us and would not come to the wedding. We ended up marrying at my own synagogue in Dublin.

The marriage came under strain. When it finally collapsed I began questioning all my connections to Judaism and to other Jews. I came to doubt whether I was a Jew in God's eyes. It was all that mattered to me. I became chronically depressed and unable to hold down a job. My peers were passing me by, starting families and building careers. I was going nowhere. I became obsessive and aggressive, focusing my frustration on people who did not deserve my wrath. I was a liability to everyone. I tried to take my own life and even messed that up, but promised my parents I would never attempt it again.

Then one night I was sitting on my own drinking a Diet Coke in a pub in Leeds, where I was staying with my brother. The pub was packed. A beautiful young Indian woman asked if I minded her sitting down beside me. I watched her unravel a nan bread wrapped in tinfoil. It looked delicious.

'Would you like some?' she asked.

I shyly declined, but soon found her pushing a portion of it towards my mouth. It was the nicest bread I have ever eaten. Her deep brown eyes penetrated mine as I ate her nan bread. Her smile made my heart race. We were soon talking excitedly about Indian food, which led to exchanges about each other's life stories. Within a week we were lovers.

Seema was one of very few people who could protect me from myself. She knew how to handle me when I was suffering from the worst ravages of depression. Wallowing in her love, I failed to notice her problems, except those that directly affected me, such as lack of money or the way she would distance herself from me sometimes.

For a while I thought the wheeze in her chest was from cigarette smoking. Then I discovered a roll of well-used tinfoil under our bed. For years she had been smoking 'off the foil' and her respiratory system was wrecked. I was *determined I would have her better again in a few months. But I didn't. Watching someone you love go through heroin withdrawal is one of the most harrowing things in the world. You will give up your last penny to alleviate their suffering, knowing full well that you are only pushing the problem down the river. I ended up buying her heroin when she had no money.*

Sometimes she seemed to have too much money, even when her hairdressing job had gone by the wayside. Then her friend let it slip that she was on the game. My natural instincts revolted. I had to accept that every time we made love, some man, even several men, had been there shortly before me.

My anger prevented me from seeing what she was going through. I never understood or fathomed her pain. I didn't understand heroin and the devilish grip it had on her. I didn't understand that she was sincere when she said her punters meant nothing to her. But I understood she loved me and that I loved her. I thought perhaps she would come off the heroin so I wouldn't have to share her with all those strange men.

We managed to contain things. She reduced her habit and came off the game. I was going to tell my parents about her and decided we would move back to Ireland and start afresh. Then I lost my job. Soon the money ran out and Seema became sick again. I could not bear to see her suffer, so I turned a blind eye when she went back on the game. I will never forgive myself. Maybe I should have gone out robbing to feed her habit.

I got another job, but her habit was getting bigger and bigger, so much so that my paltry income could not service it. Sometimes I thought of joining her in her habit, so that we could at least share our suffering. I did grab the foil and smoke a few lines. My low tolerance made for some wonderful experiences of well-being, mellowness and a quiet confidence – a temporary and welcoming haven from all-embracing depression. Common sense prevailed, though, when Seema caught me smoking her heroin in the bathroom. She threw it out the window and started hitting me. She yelled at me in Gujarati. Her anger was enough to convince me to stay away from what she referred to as her 'devil'. I recall crawling on my hands and knees in the rain-sodden back garden trying to retrieve her heroin. Eventually, she dragged me back into the kitchen, dried me off and hugged me.

'It doesn't matter, I'll get more tonight. I am not sick yet,' she said.

But I didn't want her to go out and sell her body for more heroin, and that time it was my fault that she had to. Over the next six months, Seema's habit went out of control. She was smoking about seven bags a day and occasionally skin-popping. Slowly but surely the smoking stopped and injecting became the norm. In about a month, her body was covered with track marks. Every now and then these track marks turned into abscesses, causing her great pain and discomfort. Her weight-loss was severe. She was now perpetually on the game, looking for funds to feed her habit. Work for me was intermittent, so we lived on the rim of penury.

Then we started again. Seema went on a methadone maintenance programme. I got a new job and Seema came off the game and went back to hairdressing. Again we considered moving to Ireland and beginning a new life. We thought about having a baby. She started to put on weight, and her confidence was returning. We spent a weekend in Scotland. I found my love again without the devil in her. We were so happy.

It was a Friday night. We were meeting at an Indian restaurant that had just opened in town. Seema was late. She usually phoned in when this happened, but there were no calls. After a while, I started to get anxious. I phoned the hairdresser's. She had left there more than two hours before. It was only a ten-minute bus ride home. I waited and waited. Then an old girlfriend called me. She had seen Seema on the beat.

I drove down to the red-light district and parked my car out of the way. I walked around for ages looking for her. Finally I saw her pulling her knickers up beside a BMW that was just pulling away. She was stoned and in a mess. At first she didn't recognize me and suggested that we do business. I pulled out my handkerchief and wiped what appeared to be semen stains from her blouse. My heart was broken. She put her arms around me, but I pushed her away. I gave her a hundred pounds and told her I never wanted to see her again.

The drive home was the loneliest journey of my life. We had been doing so well. Was I angry at her for selling her body or for going back on the gear? It was over, I knew that much. I had to leave England and start anew. I had to forget Seema. I had to be hard on her and hard on myself.

She telephoned all night.

Finally, a taxi pulled up outside the flat. I wouldn't let her in. I watched her face in the hall window, contorted with anger. She walked back to the taxi and gave me a sorrowful look that I will never forget.

I lay awake in bed that night, her scent still on the pillow. Perhaps we could begin again? She could come with me to Ireland. My father, a doctor, could help us. We would live outside Dublin, deep in the country, away from heroin. We would both work and save for a house. I'd show her that there was the possibility of another life. I finally fell asleep.

The next day I drove down to the red-light district straight after work to tell Seema I still loved her and wanted to start afresh. I found her friend Geordie, half spaced out on heroin.

'It's a bit fuckin' late to be doin' business wiv her!' said Geordie.

'Why?' I asked.

'She's down in the morgue.'

It took some persuading for me to be allowed to view her body. When I saw her, the world closed in. Two officials picked me up off the floor and offered me a cup of tea.

People are supposed to appear peaceful in death, but Seema didn't. I kept getting flashbacks of her looking at me as she got into the taxi the night before. Her beautiful dark face had lost its vividness. I was looking at an old woman of twenty-six, whose face was creased with lines of stress and anguish. They had left her mouth open. I closed it. Her flesh was cold. She was gone forever. I felt deep remorse. I could have saved her.

I drove towards home, but knew I could not face the night on my own. I knocked up my friend Eddie Moss. Close friends can sense pain without words. He sat me down in the living-room and handed me a bottle of Black and White whisky. He knew that the only way I would survive the night was by drinking my way out of it.

The autopsy recorded Seema's death as 'misadventure' due to a heroin overdose.

I buried her because nobody else would. She was not on record with the social services and her family would not acknowledge that she had existed. Only a few of us attended her funeral. Eddie had persuaded a kindly minister to allow her to rest in his parish church grounds.

I wrote her a long love note and placed it in her hands

just before the coffin lid was closed.

Two days later I was on a plane to Dublin. It was going to be hard living with my parents again, but I had to do it until I got sorted. I decided not to tell them about Seema, but they could see I was deeply depressed. They were very good to me and didn't ask questions. For once, I was in the right place. I had plenty of time to think. I had to plan a way out of sorrow and depression. I decided to tackle the problem head on.

Taxi drivers are the eyes and ears of Dublin. What better way to make contact with working girls whilst earning a living at the same time? I sat my taxi-driving test and took up employment with a well-known Dublin taxi company. I would write a book about drugs, about Seema, about 'the beat'.

2

THE BEAT

LIKE ANY CITY, Dublin has always had prostitutes. In times when there may have been little or no drug abuse, many women turned to selling their bodies on the streets as a way of alleviating horrific poverty. Some were alcoholics, usually on their last legs, desperate to find funds to procure drink.

After Kingsbridge station was built in 1845, many working girls would wait outside the railway-head looking for customers. It is not clear when the bulk of them crossed the river onto Benburb Street and Collins Barracks. There are still girls who work what is now called Heuston Station.

In the early 1900s the main area of prostitution was 'Monto', a maze of streets to the north and west of

Amiens Street railway station. By 1925 the new Free State government, under pressure from the Church and the Legion of Mary, decided to take action. In one massive police raid, over 120 girls were arrested; many eventually served prison terms for loitering and soliciting. Monto did not survive this raid.

Today there are four beats in Dublin, two for working girls and two for rent boys. This book concentrates on the areas used by working girls. By far the largest beat is around Baggot Street on the south side, a roughly triangular area of about a square mile and straddling the Grand Canal.

As the area is controlled by two Garda stations, Donnybrook and Harcourt Terrace, it is not uncommon for girls to cross the canal to avoid a statutory caution or arrest. Because of the complex layout of the streets, it is easy to find a suitable spot to conduct business without being detected. The beat is frequently patrolled by the police, who have the power to curtail the girls' work, but because of archaic laws they find it difficult to reduce overall prostitution. The girls naturally take advantage of this. Nobody in the force has a solution to the problem. The police conduct campaigns from time to time to clear out the area, but know full well that the girls will return.

Many girls work at fixed spots to attract regular customers. A regular is going to feel far more comfortable if he knows where to pick up his desired lady without having to cruise around and possibly attract the eye of the gardai.

The other beat is around Benburb Street just north of the Liffey, near Heuston Station and the Phoenix Park, at the end of a national auto route into Dublin. The codes and practices here are similar to those of Baggot Street, but the area attracts a different type of working girl and client. This beat is crime-ridden and many of the working girls are not actually in the business of sex, but only use it as a way to steal.

To be fair, there are many girls here who are content to ply their trade honestly. Until recently, the local gardai based at the Bridewell concentrated on pruning out girls who commited serious crimes like robbery or mugging, while leaving the others to their own devices. Under a recent change in policy, working girls around Benburb Street are now constantly cautioned and discouraged from doing business, and as a result many have relocated to the nearby Montpelier Hill or to Baggot Street.

Prices for sex are lower than along Baggot Street and can be bartered down, depending on how desperate the girl is to get the business. It is not uncommon to hear of a working girl from Benburb Street complaining that she had to do a 'hand job' for £10 to get enough money for a fix.

Unlike other capital cities, there seems to be little or no organized pimping activity in Dublin. Pimping is much more common in established brothels where working girls have to adhere to enforced rules and give up part of their take to the brothel keeper. On the street most girls look after themselves and often each other. There are only pimps in the sense that a working girl may have a boyfriend with a drug habit. She will go out to work to feed his habit also. This practice seems more common around Benburb Street, but is common enough in all districts.

Whereas there seems to be no focal point for prostitution in the Benburb Street area, many of the working girls at Baggot Street gather outside the Spar shop and adjoining cafés for a break, a fix or simply a cup of coffee. The pay phone just outside the Spar shop must be one of the busiest nighttime telephones in Dublin. The girls use it to contact clients, drug dealers or friends. Taxi drivers have always congregated at the Spar shop and many of the working girls know the taxi drivers in more ways than one. At any time during the course of a night it is rare to see this area devoid of working girls and taxi drivers.

One of the girls' biggest problems is finding a place to work without being detected. One friend used to mystify me; she had a hidden spot and I pestered her until she showed me where it was. We drove up to the security gates of an apartment complex and she entered the code. We drove on to a well-hidden place behind a row of garages. She had done business with a punter who lived here and taken note of the security code as he entered. She had used the place regularly ever since.

Security is never a big issue with the girls except for the more streetwise ones. Those who observe some precautions seem to escape beatings and rapes. Most girls work apart, others make sure that they always work in view of each other. Some always memorize a car registration number before going off with a punter. Others insist on sex by rear entry so that they can run off quickly if they have trouble. Many carry a variety of weapons and there have been reports of knife attacks where a girl felt threatened.

Punters

If you want to meet the punters, just drive down into one of the red-light districts of Dublin, park and watch.

The punters are all over the place.

There are basically three types of punters, those who walk around and are looking for fast 'relief', those who cruise around in cars, and those who pick up a working girl and bring her back to their house or hotel room.

I used to think I knew what a typical punter would look like. He was middle-aged, overweight and ugly. But in fact they come in all shapes and sizes, all ages, all nationalities.

The working girls, despite their need to feed very expensive habits, are quite selective about their punters, often refusing to do business with very young men or men over the age of fifty, foreigners or blacks. I know one girl who deals almost exclusively with members of the Chinese community; she claims they pay up without argument, come quickly and have small penises that do not hurt her! Another girl will not do business with young lads from the country because she feels many of them are drunk, dirty and violent, particularly when it is time to pay. Some will only do one-on-one sex, others are quite happy to partake in group sex.

Many girls have regulars they trust and rely on for steady income. These punters can actually be very good to the girls, helping them out when times are rough, and not always looking for sex in return. Some girls abuse these customers, however, ripping them off at any given chance. Others have the good sense to cultivate balanced professional relationships with their punters so they will have something to fall back on. Some girls, not prostitutes at all, will coax a prospective customer to a quiet place and threaten to attack him with a blood-filled needle. Some will have back-up, such as a boyfriend, waiting in the dark to pounce on the unfortunate punter. In most cases the victim will not report the robbery to the police, too embarrassed at having been there in the first place. Many a girl has made a small fortune out of these robberies and little has been done about it.

For a capital city, sex seems to sell cheap in Dublin. The going rates in the Baggot Street area are a little higher than on Benburb Street. On the south side prices start at £20 for a hand job, £30 for oral sex and £40 for full sex. A flat rate of £60 usually applies for a trip back to a punter's flat or hotel room.

On the north side the rates tend to vary on demand. Prices can start as low as £10 for hand relief, but are normally £15. Oral sex is usually around £20 but has been known to be as low as £10. Full sex normally sells for £30 in a car; anything after that is negotiable. Some of the working girls have been known to chase other girls out because they have brought down prices. What never ceases to amaze me is the punters' very business-like approach when it comes to haggling. Despite the obvious fact that many of the girls are desperate, a punter may take pleasure in bargaining down the price of sex from, say, £40 to £25. This is more likely to happen on Monday and Tuesday nights when business is very quiet.

And what happens when you have agreed to deal with a nice man who turns into a raving lunatic? Some of the girls have told me horrific stories about being waylaid, raped, robbed, and beaten. One young girl I know, Mary, was anally raped by a young man in a blue Toyota. She appeared in a shattered state outside the Spar shop in Baggot Street. Shortly afterwards, and despite her outstanding warrants, she took the advice of other working girls and reported the crime. It turned out that this man had raped another girl before and had attempted to do the same to a number of others. The Garda treated Mary with the utmost respect. One particular ban garda stands out, a young woman called Anne Aherne who has earned the trust of most of the working girls. Aherne handled this case (and many others) with great skill and tact. It was obvious that the rapist had to be caught quickly. The gardai had very little to go on, because there were no witnesses. But about a week after the rape, another working girl, Deirdre, mentioned to me that she had done business with a guy in a blue Toyota who 'gave her the creeps'. She had recorded his registration number. I drove down the road to Donnybrook Garda station to hand in the number. I thought that would be the end of the matter, but things took another turn about an hour later. I was driving back along Mespil Road, when Mary, Deirdre and Amanda ran out into the middle of the street and flagged me down.

'Follow that car!' Deirdre screamed.

About a hundred yards ahead of me was a blue Toyota with the same registration number I had just handed into the police. The Toyota turned suddenly down Leeson Street towards Donnybrook. He now knew that we were following him. He turned off his lights and accelerated. By the time we reached More-hampton Road I was clocking seventy miles and climb-ing, with three near-hysterical working girls in the back egging me on. They were discussing with each other what they were going to do to him when we caught him. I was presented with a small but sharp pocket knife and invited to cut off his testicles. This was getting silly. I decided to contact the police on my mobile phone. I sheepishly explained what I was doing and asked for some sort of direction. To my surprise they asked me to keep on chasing the Toyota until I could see them over-taking me. At this stage I was chasing the rapist through Milltown at about eighty miles an hour. It was in the early hours of the morning, thankfully. We were approaching the turn for Windy Arbour and I had to prepare myself for a sudden turn or hope that the

Toyota would keep on driving straight towards the Churchtown Viaduct. The Toyota turned towards Windy Arbour and I followed. I had fallen in love with my ten-year-old taxi. She had taken the corner like a racing car and the rapist must have realized by now he would not get away. About half a mile up the road, a massive Garda four-wheeler zoomed past me at about a hundred miles an hour. Within seconds the blue Toyota had stopped and the driver was apprehended. I pulled up about a hundred yards short of the scene despite protests from the girls. Deirdre pulled out what looked like an old carving knife and tried to get out of the car.

'I'm going to cut his fucking bollocks off!' she screamed.

We managed to pull her back into the car and a slap on the back of the head from Mary seemed to knock some sense into her. The last thing we wanted was to see Deirdre up on a charge for assaulting a rapist. A police-man came up to the taxi, thanked me for my co-opera-tion and asked me if we would mind returning to Donnybrook Garda station to hand in statements. To my annoyance, Deirdre was reluctant to do so because she had not made enough money that night – although she still wanted to cut the rapist's bollocks off.

The driver of the blue Toyota was charged and a sub-sequent investigation found him to be guilty under his own admission.

The girls love to talk about the punters. Some of the stories would leave you scratching your head. I remember one night a girl climbed into the taxi requesting a lift home after a hard night's work. I looked down and noticed that she had a massive stain across the top of her coat. When I enquired, she told me that a punter had ripped off his condom and tried to ejaculate on her face. She had managed to push him far enough away that most of his semen had landed on her coat. Apparently, she had agreed to sex for £40 but demanded and got £100 for ruining her coat. She was still angry when she left the guy's car though, so she turned back and gave one of its wings a good kicking. The punter drove off in a panic.

Many of the girls don't even perform sex with their punters. One girl told me that she visits an old man every week and all she has to do is sit on his lap and chat to him. He is quite happy to pay £60 for the service and she is equally content to talk to him about herself, her family and her problems. The same girl told me that another client asks her only to lie on the bed with her legs apart humming 'My Bonnie Lies Over the Ocean' while he stands naked at the other end of the room masturbating.

Other punters are simply too nervous to do anything. Many a girl has been delighted to have collected £40 for doing nothing. Some girls are more caring and will go to great lengths to arouse a nervous customer. In the long term this often pays off as the customer learns how to relax with the girl and subsequently becomes a regular.

One of the topics discussed among the girls is penis size and how ridiculous men are about it. One girl persuades a penis-obsessed punter that she can measure its true size by putting on a condom in a certain way. This involves stretching the base of the condom to a great length, placing it down the shaft of the penis and letting go. If the condom rolls off the penis altogether you are indeed small. If it stays on, you are big!

Many of the girls complain about what punters want for free, and other things which are off the shopping list completely. Most agree that men are obsessed with anal sex, and the few girls who are willing to co-operate command very high prices for it. Others complain that men cannot seem to understand that when they pay for sex, sex is all they get. Many expect petting beforehand, the kissing and caressing of intimate areas. But even when they are offered big money for it, the girls are usually not prepared to do it. The girls prefer to separate the act of sex with a stranger from intimacy.

Occasionally a working girl will brag about a hunk she has just done business with, but even in these circumstances, where there may be a powerful sexual attraction, many of the girls would not want to get intimate.

[34]

Do working girls ever fall in love with their punters? I have never heard of it, but I know that many are extremely fond of some of their regulars and often wish they had met them in another life. The very fact that a relationship starts with commercial sex seems to damn any possibility of a normal relationship. I know some of them have tried it, but ultimately they know that it could never work.

A few of the girls tell me that sometimes, for some reason, they become sexually aroused with a punter. They say that they do not fancy the punter but that something else triggers them off. Some feel a personal sense of satisfaction about having satisfied a punter and actually feeling him come to orgasm as a result of their actions. It is not that they find it sexual, but professionally they know they have done their job properly.

Other girls don't care one way or the other. They are there to make money and when they have earned enough they want to get away as soon as possible. In fact, I don't know any working girls who would say they enjoy their work. What is interesting is that many of the girls seem to develop an emotional blindness to what they are doing. It does not take a lot of imagination to see what these girls have to put up with. They have to carry out the most personal physical act possible with total strangers, often up to six or seven times a night. Many claim that they can just 'switch off' and detach themselves from what they are doing. I find that hard to believe. Crawling into the back of a total stranger's car and having sex for cash is very real.

The many brothels around the city attest that there are women who are quite happy to sell their bodies for acceptable amounts of money. But the girls on the street present a completely different picture. Their minds have been blighted by drug abuse; the need to satisfy a craving for heroin and cocaine pushes everything else in their lives out of perspective. Prostitution is the last calling-post in a desperate search for cash for drugs. So how do you switch off? Some girls have said that they develop a sort of mental numbness as time goes by. They know that what they are doing hurts them, but they cannot face it as long as they are addicted to drugs. Others are past caring, or at least give that impression. But anyone who knows these girls can see there is a double-edged pain, living with an uncontrollable and debilitating habit, and throwing the last remnants of dignity away in order to make ends meet.

Many go to the ends of the earth to maintain a level of decency away from their workplace. Many have reared children successfully in exceptionally difficult circumstances. I have one friend who plies the beat every night, gathering money to live and feed her habit. But she has managed to get her priorities right. No money is spent on drugs until her children are fed, clothed and looked after.

No matter how tired or exhausted she is, she always finds time to be with her two girls. When she cannot be with them, she is happy to pay for a trustworthy babysitter. Her house is well kept and spotless and had I not met her in my taxi, I would have never known she was a working girl or an addict.

Others maintain their dignity despite the fact that their bodies have become wasted, or they are homeless. I remember driving down Cumberland Road watching an ageing prostitute walk the footpath with an elegant gait. Her stockings were in tatters and the heel of one of her shoes was broken. It was raining heavily and much of her mascara had run down her face. But she still gave an impression of great human dignity. Despite years of drug abuse and years of working the beat she looked – at least from a distance – a very elegant lady.

Drugs

Broadly speaking, girls who are not drug addicts work the brothels and those who are afflicted work the streets. Girls in brothels cannot hide track marks; girls working the streets can and do. To my knowledge there are only three non-addicts in the Baggot Street area. One is blind and the other two are alcoholics. One of the alcoholics drinks a minimum of one bottle of vodka a day, although she always gives the impression of being perfectly sober. In the Benburb Street area I do not know of a single girl who is not addicted to some drug or other.

The most widely used drug is heroin, commonly known as 'gear'. Cocaine or 'charlie' is also used widely but it is very expensive and used more as a 'treat' rather than on a regular basis, although there are some who use cocaine and heroin regularly together. Much of the cocaine sold in Ireland is of very poor quality, and to find good cocaine is considered a very rare pleasure. More often the drug has been 'danced on' or diluted to make maximum profit for the dealer. The dilutant can range from paracetamol to Ajax scouring powder.

Other drugs widely used are 'sleepers' such as Rohypnol and Dalmane. When heroin supplies are scarce, or when an addict is on a methadone programme, these sleepers tend to be used constantly to compensate for the loss of the effect of heroin. It is particularly harrowing to see a young working girl taking a combination of sleepers and 'charlie', then using gear to 'come down'. Although reactions do vary, most users are reduced to an incoherent wreck. I have seen girls lean against a wall, slide down, turn over and roll along the pavement, finally coming to rest face down in a deep stupor. I have seen one girl spend a long time trying to light a cigarette, and end up setting herself on fire. I suspect that many girls have been attacked and raped under these circumstances.

With heroin, the biggest incentive to stay on the drug is the fear of 'sickness' if they come off it. The longer they stay on the drug, the quicker they become sick as their dependence on heroin increases. The addiction is all-enveloping. Addicts rob, lie, sell their bodies and their souls to satisfy an insatiable lust for drugs. This pursuit of gear is the reason that red light districts exist.

One girl I know survives on one 'twenty-bag' a day – about twice the volume a McDonald's sugar spoon can hold. I know another who cannot live on fewer than six twenty-bags of gear a day and likes to buy £40 worth of cocaine to finish off.

There are fundamentally two types of users: bangers and smokers. Those who inject ('bang' or 'use') are almost always graduates from the smoking school. It is distressing to see a long-time user, her body so worn and thin, littered with track marks and abscesses. One working girl I knew had no fewer than twelve abscesses on her arms, as well as several around her groin area and feet. Still, somehow she managed to find a vein two or three times a day to satisfy her habit. I have seen her inject directly into one of her abscesses, letting the pus seep out, then securing a vein underneath it. I have seen another girl 'skin-pop' straight into her buttock. This involved inserting the full length of the needle into muscle tissue and leaving it there until she got a 'hit'. Her buttocks were missing huge lumps of muscle tissue and had a surface similar to that of a ploughed field. Another girl started off smoking, progressed to banging, skin-popping and then returned to smoking. This return to smoking was no improvement; her habit had quadrupled and she was using other drugs as well.

Needle sharing is not uncommon, and neither is drug sharing. If circumstances prevent a working girl from getting fresh needles she may run the very high risk of sharing – the only means she has of getting a quick hit.

There is camaraderie among the girls and if one has had a bad night, there is a good chance that she will be 'thrown' a bag by one of her friends to hold her until she can make good again. On the other hand, many a girl has turned on another for stealing a punter when she needs just another £20 to get her to the dealer, or accused one of stealing gear as it is dished out by the dealer, or of coaxing the dealer into giving more to her over another. The chances are that the dealer really does not care who gets a bigger bag. He just wants to sell the stuff quickly and use the money to feed his own habit.

All the girls seem to wear two faces: one is friendly and one belongs to your worst enemy. Drug abuse seems to aggravate everything that makes their lives worse and

diminish the simplest pleasures in life. Love, food, conversation – all become secondary. Loyalty to friends
exists only as long as it does not hamper the search for
gear. A good dealer becomes indispensable. Friends fall
away one by one, followed eventually by family members. Ultimately, the drug addict is on her own, often
feeling betrayed and deserted. The only friends left are
those of their own ilk in a world where everything
revolves around drugs. Dublin has its own very extensive drug subculture, where traditional values are swept
aside for gear. No matter how unattractive or base a
dealer is, he is will always find a willing partner to grat-
ify him. This partner will be a drug addict too, seeking
a secure supply line for her own habit. Many working
girls set out to form relationships with drug dealers.

Smoking heroin does not leave external damage
except heavy teeth-staining, but the aluminium foil used
to convert the drug into smoke can cause major damage
to the lungs. It is easy to detect whether an addict is a
user or a smoker. You can hear a smoker's chest rattle as
she speaks, whereas a user's chest condition is less likely
to be audible. The heroin is emptied onto a piece of aluminium foil, often a chocolate wrapper. A flame-
adjustable lighter is then used underneath the foil to
heat up the heroin. When the heroin starts to liquify
from the heat and 'rolls' on the foil, the smoker inhales
the fumes it generates. The smoker's skill becomes

apparent from the number of roll lines she can get out of one fix. After inhalation she will soon be able to judge the quality of the gear.

Watching an addict smoke heroin is interesting, but straightforward, with little deviation in method or style. But when it comes to injecting, there are many veins, and thus many different points of entry. 'Banging' demands a great deal of skill, determination and experience. If she misses the vein she wants she runs the risk of injecting an artery and causing severe pain, arterial damage, infection and often massive swelling followed by painful and disfiguring abscesses. I have seen users suffer from a 'dirty' hit, where the heroin has not been mixed with the appropriate chemicals, or there is some foreign substance in the heroin that the body reacts to, usually manifesting itself in a severe case of the 'shivers'.

Before all this happens, the addict has to 'cook up' his gear. This involves placing the powder on a spoon, adding some citric acid in powder form to assist the heroin in liqufying, and heating it up by placing a lighter under the spoon until the stuff boils. More careful users use a cigarette filter to suck out any impurities as the cooked liquid rushes up the needle into the injection barrel. Each addict I have seen injecting seems to have developed her own style. Some positively enjoy the actual act of injection – often as much as the hit itself. (Some cocaine users get physical pleasure from a full 'flush', where the drug has already been injected but is immediately sucked back into the barrel and injected again. Sometimes the process is repeated several times, depending on the quality of the cocaine. A skilled user will know when to stop, as cocaine is notorious for clotting once it is mixed with blood.) The point of entry into a vein will become very numb if the user has given himself a poor hit.

I have witnessed great variations in behavioural and physical reaction to heroin. One working girl I knew invariably 'goofed off' after every hit. No matter how small or large the amount, she always collapsed almost immediately into a very deep sleep, alarming me so much that I drove her to hospital several times. Others I know display no effect at all. Some inject, carry on as normal, and then start to go goofy sometime later. Others appear to be slightly drunk, appearing a little overconfident, but lacking focus, conversing incoherently. In all cases, the pupils of their eyes are reduced to pinpoints almost as soon as the drug is administered. Indeed, many of the girls use pupil pinning as a measure of whether they need a fix or not. It is also used as a gauge of the quality of heroin that they have just put into themselves. The smaller the pupil, the better the quality of heroin and the longer it will be before they need another fix.

With cocaine, there are often few external effects.

The user sometimes feels a very pleasant rush, a feeling of being 'alive', optimistic and full of energy. Long-term effects vary from a feeling of invincibility to extreme forms of paranoia. Final effects range from docility or catatonia to deep depression. When someone uses cocaine over a long period of time, weight loss can be considerable. I have seen one young girl go from being very buxom to a shadow of herself within a few months.

Cocaine is not physically addictive in the same way as heroin. It produces a very powerful and seductive mental craving which becomes harder and harder to resist. Users have one taste and then go on a binge of trying to follow up hit after hit. Some users say that cocaine usage is a powerful sexual stimulant. I have heard stories about users being able to maintain an erection for hours while girls rub it around their clitoris and vaginal walls for stimulation.

Unlike the cocaine user, the heroin addict's biggest fear is getting sick and all the suffering that state involves. I watched one girl sneeze constantly for over an hour while her natural skin colour seemed to drain out of her body. I have seen girls shiver uncontrollably and give out icy sweats. I have witnessed their personal odour change from normal to foul in a very short period of time. It is hard to imagine what they suffer, but it is easy to see it and understand why someone in such a state will do anything for a fix. Their bowels frequently lose control, and I have seen working girls frantically seeking a private place to relieve themselves before they ruin their clothes. Human dignity, or what is left of it, goes out the window.

The fear of sickness can exceed even the craving for heroin in intensity. I have seen a girl panic at the prospect of getting sick even when there was a strong likelihood that she would find enough money to get a fix in time. Often it is not just a case of money. There are periods when a dealer cannot be found, particularly if a working girl finishes her beat in the early hours of the morning. She may have plenty of money but it's worthless if she cannot get her gear in time. I have overheard girls on their mobiles begging dealers to meet them, offering all kinds of perks including sex.

There is a rough code of honour among drug dealers. I know a few who will go to the ends of the earth to supply a regular customer who is on the verge of being sick. Some dealers will give 'lay-ons', or heroin on credit, if a girl has had a bad night. I have seen others 'throw' a bag at destitute homeless addicts, knowing that their chances of being repaid are slim.

For a girl to get to her dealer she needs a taxi driver, either one who is extraordinarily naïve or a regular who will expect payment in one form or another, but will be totally trustworthy. There are plenty of us. Many times I drove working girls to places around the city knowing full well where they were going and why. As time went by, I learned the drug dealers' routines and once even walked innocently into the middle of a police raid. I became known to many small-time dealers – and, regrettably, by the police. I have been tempted to cash in on the large amounts of money being made, but something has always stopped me. I have never sold drugs, even though I might be classified as a 'carrier'. I had trouble with my conscience about that, but I worked on the basis that if I didn't do it someone else would. I always took regular meter fares when they had it, and although I was offered sex instead, I always turned it down, because I believe that having sex with a woman who is desperate to be a low act. Other taxi drivers do demand sex in lieu of payment, and get it.

For a long period of time, the main sources of drugs were Fatima Mansions in Dolphin's Barn and St Michael's Estate in Inchicore. Recently both areas have become less popular. The vigilantes have become more successful, and the actual quality of the drugs coming out of these places has got poorer. And of course there is the issue of the Garda, but it has always been easy to evade the police. To be fair to them, no number of policemen could successfully patrol these areas. There are too many entrances and exits. Unless a guard actually catches you handing over a drug, there is very little he can do. Notwithstanding this, there is often a Garda presence in these areas, and the person most likely to be noticed is the taxi driver, with his plate and registration numbers clearly displayed.

Why don't the guards stop the taxis on the way out? Again, the police have very little to go on. If an addict got into my taxi, the first thing I asked her to do was to put the bag in her mouth. If a taxi is stopped, the addict swallows the drugs and resurrects them later from the toilet bowl. There is legislation now whereby the police can call in a doctor, but it rarely worthwhile for what are often very small amounts of heroin.

The fact is that the dealer is always on top, and if he is not an addict himself he will make a handsome amount of money on a regular basis. Security and a constant feeling of paranoia is the key. He will survive by paranoia, always watching his back, trusting nobody, and expecting quarter from no one. He will be despised by everyone – the police, the buyers, the supplier. Ultimately, he will be ratted on.

I knew one dealer who pretended to be a heroin addict because he felt it was safer in the long run. Most I came across are indeed addicts themselves and sometimes it is hard not to sympathize with them. Most of them sell simply to feed their own habit and maybe that of their partners. Non-street dealers are far harder to sympathize with. Often they are not addicts at all, but speculators making a very comfortable living off the desperate. I have unwittingly done the 'bull-run' several times. This means taking a street dealer to his or her source of supply, picking up 'weight' and returning to the street dealer's place. The last time it happened to me, I had no idea it was going on until my passenger pulled down her knickers and inserted a plastic bag up her vagina. The fare, including waiting, came to about £8. She handed me £20, fondled my penis and left the taxi. Since then I have avoided doing the bull-run, as I was actively contributing to the drugs business.

Unless you know your passengers well, you will have little idea what they are up to. But I was beginning to see the same faces again and again. I was being sucked in. Even making an effort to stay away from anything to do with drugs, there were no guarantees. Taxi drivers unwittingly transport drug addicts and drug dealers all over Dublin every day.

I have seen working girls take up drug dealing as a means of getting off the streets – usually to no avail. It always seemed more sensible to me to get off the gear first and then off the streets, but it is understandable that many girls would find prostitution more intolerable than addiction. There is only one girl I know who managed to get off the streets and get herself set up as a successful dealer. Many a girl has set out on a new career as a dealer, used up all her supplies herself because of her addiction, and had to disappear for her own safety.

Other dealers have come onto the streets to sell direct to the girls on the beat. In most cases the Garda get wise to them and chase them out. One dealer I know of evades arrest although he is well known to the police. He is so well established that the girls always know where he is going to be at any given time and can usually carry out a transaction with impunity.

Some of the most successful drug squads in the world are in Dublin, but they will be the first to tell you that they are only scratching the surface. Almost all detections are based on a 'ratting' system. Informers come and go, and if at any time there is not a proliferation of rats the police come under pressure to find more.

Heroin is everywhere in Dublin. Edinburgh and Dublin are believed to have the most serious heroin problems in western Europe. One of the standard jokes on the streets was that during a heroin drought a few years ago, it was being sold openly in Mountjoy. A prison officer was caught red-handed smuggling the stuff in. Even though he was caught, supplies were unaffected. Heroin was coming in stitched into clothes and slung over the walls.

Maybe there is a case for some form of controlled legalization. Many of the girls' lifestyles would be greatly enhanced if they did not have sell their bodies for heroin. The crime rate would be dramatically reduced and the jails would be emptied. Even the drug dealers would eventually disappear. If all an addict had to do was sign a form, walk up to clinic and take her drug, then she might get a job, pay her bills, enjoy some sort of normality. Such changes would dramatically reduce the level of crime in Dublin, over half of which is drug-related. And it would relieve some of the abject misery suffered by so many working girls on the beat.

3

SORCHA

I WAS DRIVING down Mespil Road one night when I saw a small figure jump into a bush behind the Mespil Hotel. A Garda car had kerb-crawled past the spot and slowed almost to a halt, then shot off again. After the Garda car was out of view, I did a U-turn and stopped at the spot. A pretty red-headed girl suddenly jumped out of the bush and leapt into the passenger seat of my car.

'Get the fuck outta here!'

'Where are we going?' I asked.

'Dollymount Strand.'

'I'm not looking for business,' I said.

'You're not getting any business, but I'll give you a score if you bring me there.'

I didn't argue; it had been a poor night and I had to pay my taxi rent the next day.

When I asked why she was going to Dollymount Strand, she looked incredulous. I felt stupid. It dawned on me what was happening as I parked up the taxi, and my suspicions were confirmed when she pulled a barrel and needle out of her bag. My heart started to race. When she saw the look of horror on my face, she broke into a hearty laugh. She was not going to mug me, but she was going to inject. I was appalled, but to her it was something perfectly normal. I don't know why I didn't insist she put the needle away.

She seemed to take great pride in injecting herself, as if it was an art. She told me that part of the kick was the physical act. Even when she had no drugs, she liked to inject alcohol.

'What happens?'

'I get pissed.'

'Why would you want to bang booze, when you can drink it?' I asked.

'Like I said, it's not always the drug, but how you put it into yourself.'

'So you get a kick out of puncturing a hole in your veins and pumping in some shit like heroin?'

'Don't be so hoity-toity,' said Sorcha with a little anger. 'We all have our little quirks, even you.'

'Do I?'

Sorcha ignored my question, took a deep sigh, moved her arm around the edge of my shoulder and looked into my eyes.

'You really know nothing about turn-ons, do you?' she asked.

'I haven't a clue,' I confessed. 'I just thought that the addiction would be so strong that you'd want to get it into you as soon as possible.'

Maybe I was thick or naïve, or both, but I could not see how an addict could get pleasure simply from injection. One way or another she was going to tell me.

Sorcha pushed the needle into a protruding vein. She wiggled the needle about until a small amount of blood entered the lower chamber. She pulled the plunger and her blood started to mix with the liquefied heroin. She forced the chamber down until it was empty. At this stage I thought it was all over, but she raised the plunger again, and pumped the bloody mixture in again. She repeated the process about four times. Her eyes dimmed and her speech slurred.

'What was all that about?' I asked.

'The flush.'

'The what?' Sorcha goofed off, drifting in and out of reality. It was an eye-opening experience for me; I was transfixed. She was a strong-willed girl. If I had protested, she would probably have just got out of the taxi and injected elsewhere. I did not want her to go.

[53]

The episode was not over yet; I watched her struggle to find another vein. She had saved cooked liquid heroin on her spoon for a second fix, but this time she was having problems. Soon both her arms were covered in blood and it was looking like she was not going to manage a fix. Then she hitched up her skirt and pulled down her tights. After a minute or two, she managed to inject herself in the groin. Soon she found difficulty in keeping her eyes open and her speech became halting. I was alarmed and suggested I bring her to a casualty unit in hospital. Again, she managed a hearty laugh and assured me she was only 'goofing'. I was not sure so I kept on talking to keep her awake. After a while, the goofing wore off and she seemed to revive.

That was the start of my long, loving and painful relationship with Sorcha. The minute she jumped out of that bush in Mespil Road, I was hooked. I could feel love, affection and passion for her, mixed with deep sorrow, pity and anguish. Sometimes I loved her as a woman, sometimes I was a father-figure. I was prepared to place my whole future with her.

There were many more Dollymount Strand excursions. She told me about her past. She was the product of an extramarital affair; her mother was only nineteen when she gave birth. Sorcha was pushed from pillar to post between her grandmother and her mother. Her sense of rejection was compounded by her stepfather's sex abuse; he started having sex with her when she was only six. A boyfriend introduced her to heroin and she became pregnant by him at the age of fifteen. Another relationship ended with her lover stabbing her just above her left eyelid. Her ageing grandmother found it hard to control her and she soon left her home town of Wicklow for Dublin. By this stage, she was totally 'strung out' on heroin and her only source of income was prostitution. Initially, she worked the Benburb Street area, but soon 'graduated' to Baggot Street.

I knew I couldn't ask her to get off drugs. It would take some time and it would take even longer for her to acclimatize to normal life. But I was in love with her and I would do anything. Many a time we talked 'happy families' and what it would be like to be together in a normal life. We decided we wanted a baby and set about the task. Within a few days she told me that she was pregnant. I was over the moon. I had always wanted a child, and the woman I loved was going to give me this great gift. Then gossip came back that she was not pregnant at all. Not having a high regard for working-girl gossip, I disregarded it, but it was persistent, and several gentle warnings from friends told me that the whole pregnancy was a charade. I checked with my father, a doctor, and he agreed it was unlikely that she was pregnant. It was became obvious that Sorcha was lying and had found herself a new man. I was hurt and I still hurt.

What was she after – money? She would have got that anyhow.

Sorcha never quite left my head. The other girls told me how she was getting on. She had ingratiated herself with a punter called Dennis who professed that he was not after her for sex, but would be happy to supply her with a flat and drugs when he could get them. Dennis was made out to be some tough guy but when I spoke to him he struck me as a reasonable man. I told him that Sorcha had moved back to her grandmother's and was starting to lead a new life. I asked him to back off, and he agreed to, happy that Sorcha was sorting herself out.

Months later I saw her walking the beat. I discovered that she had shacked up with a junkie taxi driver after her boyfriend had been jailed. She had trouble with a policeman who declared his undying love for her, expressed by harassing her on the beat and feeling her up.

Then one night she telephoned me. She had nowhere to sleep, no money and just enough heroin to get by. I drove around Dublin trying to find a bed and breakfast for her, to no avail. She ended up staying the night with me at my flat. She was exhausted but offered to have sex with me. I interpreted it as some form of payment and said no. I could only make love to a girl like Sorcha, I couldn't simply have sex.

She goofed off in the bath and I woke her so she wouldn't drown. Her naked body was shivering. I dried her and put her to bed. She turned around and cuddled up to me and we both fell into a deep sleep. I remember waking up and looking at her beautiful sleeping face. All the pain and anguish of drug addiction and working the streets had disappeared.

We arranged to meet the next day, but she never turned up. I found out later that she had run off with a drug dealer and was selling heroin out of St Michael's Estate in Inchicore. Occasionally I would get a telephone call, but there was always an ulterior motive and I declined to meet her, although every time I spoke to her it hurt.

Sorcha started to deteriorate. She became very thin, unwashed and smelly. One day, I brought her into town and kitted her out with new clothes. I promised her that I would look after her, if only she would at least try to find some direction in life. About three weeks later she was still wearing the same clothes, but now they were covered in cigarette holes and blood stains. She had become desperately thin from an accelerating cocaine habit, a heroin habit and lack of food. She started eating her clothes and this led to a stomach disorder. Her skin was sheet white and she always seemed to be very cold. I had visions of her overdosing or dying in pain. She moved back in with the taxi driver addict.

I visited her frequently, buying her clothes, food and cigarettes and giving her small amounts of money. She contracted scabies and, as she scratched herself, her body became covered in small sores. I asked her to see a doctor about this and she agreed. But we were both tired of life, and even talked of a suicide pact.

I finally persuaded her to return to her grandmother, knowing she would still go back on the streets to get money for heroin, but at least having a base, safe with someone who truly loved her.

One night she was arrested and brought to Harcourt Terrace Garda station. A detective let her telephone me. When I arrived, she was sitting in a cell crying. I begged the detective to let her out, but the paperwork had already been processed. She was up in court in the morning and faced custody for her string of outstanding warrants. Fortunately, the judge was receptive to her case and I was allowed to pay for her bail under certain conditions. She had to return to Wicklow and attend several drug-related meetings. She had to register with a doctor and go on a methadone programme. The detective had agreed to these terms and Sorcha was given a last chance. She was to report back to court early in the new year. She was not to come into Dublin between the hours of 8 p.m. and 8 a.m. There would be no more chances.

At first, she found it difficult to be back in Wicklow, but slowly she managed to organize her life. One of the most difficult things about coming off drugs and trying to lead a normal life is the enormous vacuum it creates. But Sorcha had aspirations and targets. She yearned for the day when she would be reunited with her daughter. We talked about setting up home together with her daughter and having another baby. She went to see a social worker, who attempted to meet the child's father. He didn't turn up. It was a setback, but ultimately this would work in Sorcha's favour in the courts. Our age difference was vast but she often told me that it never mattered to her. Her mother said she thought I was a pimp; Sorcha put her right.

Not so long ago, we spent the night together. She told me that she'd never go on the streets again. She wanted a fresh start and she wanted me to be part of it. I felt elated. The following night, I had a phone call from another working girl; Sorcha had been seen getting into the junkie taxi driver's car after being on the beat. I phoned her mother just to be sure. Her mother asked me to bring her back to Wicklow. I cornered the other taxi on Pembroke Road and would not move until she got into my car. We had a terrible row, and I ended up slapping her across the back of her head. I will regret that for the rest of my life, but I had told her mother that I would bring her home and I did.

If ever anyone gave me experience of being with a drug-abuser, Sorcha did. All she had was heroin, so I shared it with her, once. It frightened her, and for a long time she would not even talk about drugs to me. She announced one day that even if we were to get closer, we were not to have sex at all. I understood this and accepted it.

When I am lonely now, I think of her with her head on my shoulder, sleeping, with all the strain and pain gone out of her face.

The girls keep me informed of her movements. Her grandmother died and Sorcha was distraught. Her weight-loss became very serious and she was losing the power of her right leg, a result of constantly injecting into the groin. I sent her a letter telling her that I was still here for her. I got no response. Sorcha hasn't been seen on the beat for many months but has confined herself in her friend's home, occasionally emerging to visit her daughter – the one bright light in her life.

4

AMANDA

A CERTAIN VICE SQUAD DETECTIVE agreed with me recently that Dublin is an unusual major city in that it has no pimps on the streets. But what is a pimp? If it just means someone who lives off the immoral earnings of working girls, then Dublin's streets are awash with pimps. During my sojourn in the vice business I have met a few, and one in particular nearly ruined my life.

Early in the night I had parked my taxi outside the Spar in Baggot Street and had got a cup of tea. There was hardly anyone about except for a stunningly beautiful blonde with huge blue eyes. She gave me an innocent smile. She looked very young and healthy. I overheard her chatting to the man behind the counter. She had a faint Geordie accent. I went back to the car as it started to pour down. I was just about to nod off when I heard someone tapping on the window. It was the blonde from the shop. She asked me to take her to Maynooth; as it was outside the Dublin taxi area we quickly agreed on a fare. Soon we were in deep conversation and it turned out that she was a working girl and a drug addict.

We seemed to get on well and she understood that I was not looking for business. I'd quickly found out that if you are transporting a working girl, it makes no difference if you tell them you are not looking for business, because they will not believe you. Understandably, to them all men are life-support machines for their willies. I fancied her like mad, but I also knew that even if there was a hope of getting involved, it would mean great pain for us both. Anyway, her friendship felt nice and safe to me, and over time we developed a close bond.

She told me about her distressing childhood in England, her move to Ireland, and losing her babies to the social services because of drug abuse. She lived with her two brothers since her mother had abandoned them and gone to the west of Ireland. Her younger brother, whom she adored, was also at risk of being taken by social services and she lived in fear of this. He was fostered and I spent a lot of time with Amanda consoling her and assuring her it was for the best.

She regularly spoke about her clients, about the harrowing times when she was raped or beaten up. One client kept on coming up, someone called Bob. All I knew about him was that he was a taxi driver in his late sixties, married with a daughter and grandchildren. Bob was very kind to Amanda and, to my knowledge, still is. He buys her clothing, food and drugs, and over a year ago he set up a flat for her, paying the deposit and the rent.

One night, Amanda came running to me in some distress. Apparently Bob had become quite obsessed about my relationship with her and wanted it to end. He had given her an ultimatum. No more drugs, food, shelter, or money, unless I disappeared. He refused to believe that there was no sex between Amanda and me. Part of Bob's deal with Amanda was that sex had to be paid for and was always referred to as 'doing business'. I suppose it started as a simple case of unwarranted jealousy. But as far as I was concerned, there was nothing to be jealous of. Bob was a client of Amanda, and Amanda was a close, personal friend, someone I loved. Amanda was understandably distressed, and I knew I had to do something to sort this problem out. She agreed to let me try to reason with him.

I approached Bob on Baggot Street, car window to car window. He told me to stop ' fucking his woman'. I assured him that whatever relationship I had with Amanda was none of his business and the best thing he could do was stop trying to blackmail her. He accelerated away, threatening to kill Amanda, and I pursued him in my taxi. The chase finally ended at a petrol service station where he arranged to have himself locked into the shop by the attendant. Many obscene gestures were exchanged through the shop window until suddenly, with a nod from Bob to the attendant, the automatic door opened. I rushed in and started shouting at him. He accused me of being a pimp and I grabbed him by his shirt collar. The moment I made contact, he looked up at the CCTV camera. I let go immediately and walked out, deciding to drive back to the Spar on Baggot Street, grab a cup of tea and try to calm down. About twenty minutes later, four burly gardai arrested me and hauled me out of my taxi. They handcuffed me behind my back, creating a public spectacle for my fellow taxi drivers now crowding outside the shop.

Over the next five hours I was strip-searched and then questioned about every aspect of my life. The inside of the cell was unspeakably filthy. The concrete bed was covered by a blanket smeared with faeces, and the open toilet stank of stale urine.

After being released I did some research on Bob and found out that two girls were beaten up on his orders for having ripped him off of a small amount of cocaine. One had been nearly strangled and then dragged along the pavement by the hair. The front part of her body was covered in small lacerations. Of course the attackers disappeared despite the best efforts of the police to find out who did it. Both girls were reluctant to make an issue out of it because of outstanding loitering warrants, and the whole episode was soon forgotten. Curiously, Bob was never questioned about the incident.

One night a known drugs supplier got into Bob's taxi outside the Spar shop and handed him a large bag of what appeared to be heroin. I was standing with two of the working girls when this happened. The girls were flabbergasted. How could he get away with this? Was Bob being protected by the police? Accepting the working girls' reputation for very imaginative gossip, I would not believe these rumours, but something was amiss.

I subsequently discovered that the police were conducting a drugs investigation on Bob. I spoke to my Garda contacts and they said Bob was very clever at getting out of situations by using a female carrier who inserted the drugs internally. There was generally too little evidence to build a case. But Bob had been operating in a very small area for a year and a half, trading drugs openly from his taxi. How could they not investigate him? They did not want me to know about it. In retrospect, I understand why. My amateurish attempts at bringing Bob to the attention of the authorities might have compromised their investigation.

At this stage, Bob decided to conduct an open war against me, informing the police that I was a pimp and drug dealer. Many of the girls came to the rescue, assuring the police that this was untrue. Worse was to follow. I got a phone call from the boss of my taxi company to return to the office immediately. Bob had paid them a visit and told them that I was using the taxi to pimp girls and sell drugs. They had received a letter detailing my illicit activities. Fortunately, my bosses decided to accept my side of the story.

I kept on getting anonymous telephone calls threatening to have my head smashed, citing people I knew. I was getting angrier and more frightened by the day. Bob had bragged that he would have me off the road as a taxi driver in weeks, jailed for assault and in tatters. At one stage he phoned me up seeking a 'truce'. I assured him that I had no interest in him whatsoever so long as Amanda was not harmed in any way and that any time she wanted to leave him, he would let her go. He agreed to this, but confidently told me that she loved him and would stay with him.

Some time later, I received a telephone call asking me to go to a house in Dundrum where Amanda was staying for a few days. When I saw her, I started to cry. This beautiful girl was reduced to a skeleton. Her arms and legs were covered in sticky abscesses and she looked like she was dying. I put my arms around her and we just held each other. One of her friends had managed to talk her into taking antibiotics and she told me that her abscesses were slowly healing.

'Are you alright?' I finally asked.

'He's given me another hiding,' she said, bursting into tears.

She lifted up her left arm to show me bruises.

'I'm going to kill him,' I said.

'No, you're not,' said Amanda. 'You're not going to go near him. You won't win. In the end, he'll get me, then you, then your family.'

'Then you have to leave him,' I said.

'You know I can't, at least not yet.'

I told her that when she was ready I would get her a flat and give her a start, but that she had to go on a programme before it was too late. I am still waiting for an answer.

I was taking another working girl, Penny, to work one day after picking her up in Whitehall. At Griffith Avenue I saw Bob following us. He drew up next to me and threatened to cut Penny's throat and have me locked up. I told him if he didn't go away I'd tell his wife what a bastard he was. He went berserk. His pupils were enlarged and his nose was sore and runny. He was on cocaine and showing the classical symptoms of 'invincibility'. The lights changed and I drove on towards the city centre. At South King Street he managed to block me off. I jumped out of the car and told Penny to stay put. She was petrified. I went up to Bob, who was scrambling in his glove box, and pulled the keys out of his ignition so I might make my escape. But he got out of the car, swung me around and punched me in the face. I swung his arm around his back and forced him down onto the street. As he was getting to his feet, Penny and I left.

The following morning I was awakened by a telephone call telling me that 'Hitler had the right idea' and that I should join the 'rest of my cousins'. The threatening calls continued for about three weeks.

I drove over to Amanda's house. We had a long embrace in the hall and then went upstairs into her one-roomed flat. Sitting at the other end of the room was a working girl called Gillian who I didn't fully trust. But Amanda said she was sound and I had no choice but to talk to her in front of Gillian. Amanda was surprised by my stories of Bob's antics but said that she would try to make him stop. I told her I was tired of the whole thing and just wanted a normal life. We went back downstairs. I put my arms around her and told her that I would keep my promise to give her a new start in life. She was not ready yet.

'Amanda, the place is filthy,' I said.

'I know.'

'This isn't like you. You used to be so fussy.'

'I just don't care anymore.'

'But I do,' I said.

'I know.'

I lifted her up into my arms and sat with her. She nuzzled her face into my chest.

She was very tired and her double addiction to cocaine and heroin was taking its toll. She had become painfully thin and her arms were still covered in sores from injections. I had to leave a means of escape for her, even though I knew in my heart of hearts that she would stay there so long as the cocaine and heroin kept flowing. I left knowing that she would implore Bob to back off, but I wasn't too sure about Gillian.

A few days later I was waiting at an empty rank by Stephen's Green early in the evening. I was dozing when I heard somebody get in the back. Before I could ask where we were going, something sharp and pointed was pressed into the base of my skull. I could hear breathing. I thought I was going to die. I did not lift my eyes up, but could just see a bare outline of a head in the rear-view mirror. The assailant jumped out and made his way across the road and down an alleyway towards Mercer Street. I saw his blue-striped track suit, closely cropped hair and woollen hat. He was putting something down his trousers when he disappeared around the corner. Suddenly I vomited all over the steering wheel and the dashboard. I drove home in my filthy car, crying and thinking about my parents, my brothers and my late grandfather.

Recently I found out that Amanda's flat had been

raided and she was caught with an ounce of heroin. Bob would have got a suspended prison sentence, at best a slap on the wrists. But Amanda has a record and is a known working girl, drug dealer and addict. She is looking at four years.

I sent Amanda a birthday card this year with the message 'I'm waiting'. A few days later, I received a lovely card back with the message, 'One day, I promise.'

5

KARIS

KARIS IS AN ADOPTED CHILD from a middle-class home in Clontarf. When her father died she was aged eleven, and her world seemed to cave in. There was always friction between her mother and her brother.

She fell in with a boyfriend who was no good for her and who ultimately led her into taking heroin. She had a son when she was seventeen, but gave the child up to her mother as she realized that her heroin addiction was beginning to rule her life. It was not long before she turned to prostitution.

I remember her describing to me her first 'car job'. It was an old man. She just lay there and let it happen and cried and cried. There would be many more punters, some who would look after her well, others who would abuse her. She has built up regulars and, although she works the streets, she does not have to all the time. Unlike the other girls, she does not stick strictly to the traditional beat area, but wanders around the periphery. Her regulars know where to find her but she does not have to compete with the other girls and she has less of a chance of attracting attention from the police.

In the two years that I have known Karis, she must have moved ten times, occasionally to a hotel or bed and breakfast.

Like her friend Bridget, she is expert at getting people to feel sorry for her while bleeding them dry. I fell victim to this. Many a time I would 'loan' her money after she'd had a bad night, knowing full well that I would never see it again.

I became very close to her on a strictly platonic basis until I finally saw she was using me. I didn't like being known as Karis's taxi-driver. Mad rumours spread that we were living together or that she was carrying my baby.

During thin times, I let her stay in my flat, but soon got fed up with her. When she injected herself she would leave blood everywhere. She insisted on smoking when she goofed off and would set her clothes on fire. She never seemed to change her clothing in the normal way, but would discard what she was wearing for something she had just bought. Thus, there are literally sacks full of clothing belonging to Karis all over town. I still have some of her items in my wardrobe.

Recently she moved in with a young man she met at work. George was a straightforward guy and it was clear he loved her and wanted to give her a start in life. It was not long, however, before he was taking heroin himself and partly supporting Karis's habit. Karis came off the game for a while, but George realized that his wage could not support two habits and she was soon back on the beat. He eventually left. She couldn't pay the rent and lost the flat. Her neighbour Janey decided to take her in until she found a new home, but that did not last long either. At first things were okay. Then Janey found blood spots on her baby's pillow. Cigarette burns led to arguments. Janey's boyfriend turned against Karis. The final straw came when Karis left Janey's baby alone in the flat while she went out searching for heroin. Janey telephoned me up in a rage. She was going to batter her. I told her not to hurt Karis, but just order her to leave.

Karis has been staying at a hostel since, while walking the beat. For a while she befriended a taxi driver who used to drive her all over the place like I did. But I haven't seen them together recently. Maybe the taxi driver realized he wasn't on to a winner.

Karis used to live with another girl whose father was a policeman. I arrived one night to find her beating up her friend. I managed to prise them apart and drag Karis off in my taxi. The following night her flatmate's father phoned demanding I deliver Karis to him. I refused. That may have been the beginning of my troubles with the authorities.

Later I learned to my horror that Karis moved in with Amanda and Bob. I took it as a direct dig against me and felt that my worst feelings about her were confirmed.

One busy Saturday night I threw out two drunks from my taxi and got thumped in the face for the effort. A little later, tired, I parked outside the Centra on Dorset Street, locked all the doors, put the seat back and nodded off. I was woken by a persistent tapping on the front passenger window.

At first I thought it was a fare, but soon saw that it was Karis. I swore that I would never have anything to do with her again, but her big brown eyes, and her sheer cheek in approaching me, changed my mind. I opened the door and she got in, greeting me with a very muted 'Hi'. I responded in kind. There was a long pregnant silence, sprinkled with numerous exchanges of flushed, embarrassed smiles. The conversation came along slowly like an old steam train building up power after being stationary for a long time. We finally moved on to the serious stuff.

'So what the hell are you doing living in Bob's place?' I asked.

'I had to live somewhere, and I know what you're thinking. It had nothing to do with you.'

I believed her. A working girl would never be foolish enough to reject a place to live in, whatever about the politics. She had a right to look after herself first and foremost. We talked for ages and ploughed through all the hurts and upsets until we became friends again. We reduced the tone of the conversation to slagging off everyone we knew. It was like we had never fallen out.

'You got your hair cut,' I accused her.

'It's my hair,' she said.

'Your bum has got bigger.'

'It will never be as big as yours.'

We gave each other a long hug and she got out of the taxi. I watched her walk off, with that self-conscious walk girls have when they know they're being watched. Karis was back.

6

UNA

NOT MANY GIRLS have the courage to wear fishnet tights without a skirt, not even a working girl, but Una does. Full of colour no matter what her circumstances, she always meets you with a smile.

Una is from Bawnogue on the outskirts of west Dublin. She was born into a family where crime was second nature to her siblings. I first met her when she jumped into my taxi with what I assumed was her boyfriend. We were heading out to Coolock. The man asked me to stop at a shop on Dorset Street. As soon as he walked in, Una ordered me to go. I drove off. She produced a wad of money and was gleefully counting it. It didn't take me long to figure what was going on. Una was a working girl and she had either 'dipped' this man, or had taken payment off him and done a runner. I was party to a crime, however unwittingly.

'You're Dave, aren't you?' she asked.

'How do you know?'

'The girls told me all about you. The taxi drivers call you the whoremaster because you're always shunting us girls around.'

'Do you believe that crap?' I asked.

'No.' But she had a wispy expression as if she was not quite sure.

'Look, I'm no whoremaster, right?'

'Okay!' she responded, this time a bit louder. This was followed by a sexy grin that could only belong to her. I felt a little embarrassed and sheepishly grinned back.

'So, do you want to do business then?'

'No way!' I retorted, a little too strongly.

More gently, I said, 'The whoremaster is too knackered. He's had too many shags today. And he thinks you're such a nice girl that he would feel guilty taking thirty quid off you just to satisfy your raging lust for him.'

Her mouth opened and closed several times. Did she get the joke?

'On yer bike, some whoremaster you are!' she answered.

'Okay, because we've made friends, I'll settle for twenty quid, but I want the money before we strip,' I said.

'Actually, it's forty quid and I wouldn't have sex with you if you were the last man on earth, never mind paying for it,' she said.

'You charge forty quid?' I said with mock incredulity. 'Who do you ride, the royal family?'

'Naw, they don't pay enough. Anyway that Charlie fella's ears are too big.'

I drove Una to a basement flat on the Rialto end of the South Circular Road. She was full of life and mischief. It turned out that she had become addicted to heroin at the age of fourteen and had then got into a relationship with a dealer. He ended up beating her, so she went out on the game. Since then she has hovered between dealers and being on the game, a classic case of the itinerant working lady. Nobody is quite sure where she is living at any given time. We became good friends over a period of months and I quickly learned that her cheerful disposition hid a great deal of sadness.

Although Una is tough by nature and well used to street life, she sometimes has high moral aspirations and becomes bitterly disappointed when she feels let down. Her regard for her clients seems to be very low. She will do anything to avoid sexual contact and get the money off them as quick as possible. She told me that she was once picked up by a middle-aged businessman and brought back to his apartment in Foxrock. He wanted to be tied up naked. Una obliged, robbed him of his money and left him there for his wife to untie him.

'You just left him there for his wife?' I asked.

'So?'

'What do you mean, so?'

'He's only a fucking punter.'

'He paid you good money.'

'Well, if he wanted a happy marriage without coming to a whore, he should have got his wife to tie him up.'

'But you robbed him.'

'So?'

'Well, that is wrong, dishonest and not becoming of a nice girl like you.'

'Who the fuck do you think you are, mister judge almighty?' she said. 'You make a lousy jokester, whore-master and judge.'

'I'm none of them.'

'I know, but you make one hell of a pain in the bollocks.'

She knelt over and gave me a kiss. I suspected that she really did understand me, but didn't like being caught out in an argument.

Some time later I was walking out of the Spar shop on Lower Baggot Street in the early hours and observed a drunk lying face-down on the pavement. Una appeared from nowhere and walked over to him, rolled him face up and took his wallet. I grabbed her and pulled her into a shop doorway.

'Give us the wallet,' I demanded.

'Fuck off.'

I grabbed the wallet and stuffed it into the drunk's trouser pocket, making sure to rouse him at the same time. Una walked off in a temper and I laughed, since her walk says, 'Here is my head, my arse is coming later.'

After about ten minutes she returned and walked up to me as if nothing had happened. She had a large sack of clothing hidden in a skip nearby and she wanted me to mind it for her for a few days. It was pitiful seeing this sackful of clothing and personal items. It was all she had.

I didn't see her for months and ended up consigning her sack to the attic. Then one Tuesday morning I got a telephone call. Una was hardly coherent, crying hard. I picked her up on Adelaide Road, and she told me that a policeman who used to be a regular punter had given her a hiding and taken her money. He threw her out on Sandymount Strand and she had walked all the way back. She wanted to stay the night and telephone her mother in the morning to see if she would let her come home. I couldn't refuse. I put her in the box room and went to bed.

I awoke about an hour later to hear yelping noises. I jumped out of bed, thinking she must be having a nightmare or something. To my surprise, she was playing games on my computer and thoroughly enjoying herself. I went back to bed again and woke up a little later to find her arms being wrapped around my chest from behind and her head snuggling in between my shoulder blades. At first I was surprised, and, like any man, aroused. But Una didn't want sex and I understood. She just wanted to be close to someone. If we'd made love I would have just looked like another punter to her. We slept peacefully.

When I awoke the next day she was gone. My instincts told me that there was no point in looking for her. She'd simply turn up again when she wanted to.

I bumped into her in town a few months later. She was with a tall young man who looked about ten years younger than her. She was stoned out of her head. What alarmed me was the scratch marks on both her cheeks. She told me that she had been in a fight with one of the working girls on Benburb Street. She had gone with her on a job and the other girl had taken the money and done a runner, leaving Una with two angry young men wanting sex. She had to oblige or be beaten, and when it was all over, she spent the rest of the day looking for the other girl. She found her in Le Fanu Park in Ballyfermot and proceeded to give her a good hiding in front of several spectators. Una seemed to come off the worst, though: her face was in a right mess.

Just before Christmas, I got a call from her.

'You dirty scumbucket,' she screamed down the phone.

I tried to get out of her what she was angry about. One of the girls had told her that I'd said she had fleas. Of course it was a load of rubbish. I would never tell anyone she had fleas except her. But she didn't believe me. She was going to have me murdered and have my house burnt down. I assured her that my house did not belong to me, and I didn't mind anyway.

'Look, Una, phone me when you're rational again,' I said.

I switched off my mobile phone. When I switched it on again hours later, there were four messages from Una in declining degrees of severity, from 'I'm going to have you battered' to 'Dave, please get in touch with me, I'm up at the flat.'

I thought it was best to let things simmer down for a few days.

The following weekend, I awoke to a tapping on the window downstairs. It was Una, wearing her fishnet tights and not an awful lot else. I let her in, deciding to put on one of my angry/serious looks.

Before I could open my mouth, Una had jumped the gun.

'Do you like my tights?'

'They're very sexy,' I said, feeling a bit flustered.

To my horror, she bent over, pulled her tights off and mooned me.

'Now what do you think of that?' she asked, her pretty face turned at an angle to her bare bottom.

For once I was lost for words. She dressed herself quickly. In an instant she put her arms around my neck and hugged me until I had to catch my breath.

'Friends?' she asked, her deep blue eyes looking into mine.

'Friends,' I answered, giving her a quick kiss on the lips.

'Can I do a turn-on in your flat?" she asked hopefully.

'No fucking way,' I said. The last thing I needed was a working girl smoking heroin in my home.

Still, she stayed about an hour and told me that she was selling gear to stay off the street. The usual stuff about getting clean arose, but I knew it was only talk.

For a long time, she seemed to have disappeared altogether. She may have got into another relationship with a dealer, a man who would have heroin all the time. Janey had told me that she was looking to score in Fatima Mansions and found Una stoned out of her head and wandering about in men's pyjamas. She added that she'd lost a huge amount of weight.

That very morning about 5.30 a.m. I was driving through Ballyfermot on a radio call. I noticed a middle-aged lady standing at a bus stop wearing a warm overcoat, mittens and clutching a carrier bag. It was Una's mother waiting for the first bus to be on time for her cleaning job in the city. I'd no doubt in my mind that her mother had done the best she could. I'd no doubt that mother and daughter had a great love for each other. But nothing could stop the drugs from ruining it.

I know Una well. She has a huge heart and when you pull away the negative debris that has littered her life – the heroin, cocaine, the E-tablets, the game, the lovers, the well-meaning people, the bleak horizons – you find a lovely woman crying out for liberation.

The uniforms finally lock her up. She is worse inside than outside. She gets involved in a quasi-lesbian relationship with another addict and everything always ends in a heroin-induced haze. She knows no better. She once told me she got more hassle out of the police than out of clients.

The police seem to be pursuing a policy of intermittent harassment in order to keep the number of working girls to a minimum on the street. I worry that Una could be dead in ten years from the pressure of life, or end up insane, hospitalized, or just plain worn-out, willing to do anything with anybody so she can score.

The outlook is bleak, but I believe she could be

saved. For a start she and the other girls could go under 'contract' with the Powers that Be. Some years ago in Bradford the police moved all the working girls to a non-residential area of the city. A loose contract came into force: if the girls stuck to the specified area, the police would not prosecute them, and it had to be a drugs-free zone. It has worked pretty well and could work here.

Una is not harming anyone except herself. If the establishment was more understanding and less damning she would have half a chance, and so would the rest of the girls.

7

BRIDGET

BRIDGET HAS HUGE, blue, innocent-looking eyes, a full mouth and a pale complexion. When she goes to work, she coats her frizzy hair in lacquer and pulls it back into a tight bun. That, and her little black frock coat, makes her resemble an underage outer-space caricature granny. At other times, her small lean figure makes her look like a little girl, which helps to attract punters.

Bridget is from a respectable middle-class Drimnagh family. She grew up with two older brothers, who doted on her. Their two-bedroom semi was converted to accommodate the new arrival. As a child, she was the centre of attention. In her early teens, she got a boyfriend, much older than her, who was from a well-known drug-dealing family. He introduced her to heroin. She idolized him, but he treated her roughly. I heard that once he held her by the ankles over a top-floor balcony in Fatima Mansions as a punishment for stealing some of his heroin.

Bridget has made many enemies, particularly among working girls. She has gained a reputation for poaching business and intimidating punters. Some of the drug dealers do not like her either, as she has been known to steal bags of heroin from under their noses.

She seems to get on well with the police, though, and there are those who think that she gets on too well with them. It is said that she is a rat, pointing the police in the right direction.

Bridget has a tremendous talent in acting the 'little lost girl'. But sometimes, she *is* a little lost girl and suffers like the others from drug sickness, beatings and abuse. On one occasion she was raped and had the courage to go to the police and ask them to start an investigation, despite her outstanding warrants. That investigation did lead to an arrest.

On another occasion, her mother found her lying face down on the floor of her bedroom with a needle in her buttock. Not for the first time, her mother threw her out of her house. I let her stay in my flat for a few days. Despite persistent rumours that Bridget was an accomplished thief, her behaviour in my flat was excellent. She cheerily took part in all the chores and it was a pleasure to see her happy for a while.

She gathered the courage to telephone her mother from my flat.

'Ma, it's Bridget.'

'What do you want?'

'Can I come home, Ma?'

'No.'

'Please, Ma, I'm on the streets, I've nowhere to go.'

'It's no good, Bridget, you'll just go back on those drugs again.'

'Please, Ma!' she started to cry out loud.

'No Bridget, it's no good.'

There was no conversation for a while, just Bridget crying loudly into the telephone. Then there was silence.

'Please Ma, just for a few days, I need a rest. I promise no drugs, I just want to go to bed.'

A further silence was followed by an 'okay' from her mother.

Bridget looked up at me as she put the receiver down. Her huge eyes were rimmed with red. Her mother was the only person who could have that effect on her. Now, at least for a short while, she would be away from the pimps, the punters, the drug dealers and the police; she was going home.

I felt sorry for her mother, saddled with a daughter with a crippling heroin habit, on the game and up to all sorts of misdemeanours. Her mother seemed to place her faith in God and turned to the Church for solace, comfort and help. But so far the Church has not helped Bridget.

Things must have become more unbearable for her mother when she learned that Bridget's eldest brother had become strung out on heroin. Bridget and Fraser started dealing and were making quite tidy profits for a while. Bridget was able to come off the game and live at home again. But soon the vigilantes struck, burning Fraser's car to a shell. This was quickly followed by a police raid and soon Bridget was on the game again.

She lives for the day when her boyfriend comes out of prison. Her mother has stopped accepting his telephone calls, dreading the time when he takes up with her daughter again.

Bridget is very popular with the taxi drivers who congregate around the Spar in Baggot Street in the early hours. She always manages to get a free ride home, often after a free cup of tea and a cake. The taxi drivers love her because she does not put on any airs and readily admits that she is a working girl. But the better-informed ones don't like or trust her and, using her best social skills, Bridget will avoid any person who may take issue with her. There always seems to be somebody after her. Many a time I have seen her come out the worse for wear after a fight with one of the girls. Bridget always works on her own, never staying in one place for very long.

She also has a sentimental side to her character, becoming blindly devoted to one or two others for a short time. The very fact that she has decided you are the best person in the world comes at a price. You are expected to be an instant cash fund, and when it becomes clear to her that you are not prepared for that, you incur her wrath. Rumours start abounding that you are a drug pusher, fancy little girls, demand sex for transport and so on. I steer clear of Bridget. Other taxi drivers have not, and it is costing them.

Unlike relatively normal people, Bridget would not cross the street to talk to you, but stays put and shouts, irrespective of whether you are engaged in conversation with someone else or not. Her screeching catcalls in her shrill Dublin accent are renowned right across the beat, and the other girls take great joy in mimicking her.

Where someone else might say: 'Hi, Elaine, can I have a word with you?' Bridget would yell from the other end of the street: 'Elayin, c'mere, will yeh? Elayin, d'ye fuckin' heeer me? Youse robbed me punter, ya fuckin' pox!'

The unfortunate victim would eventually give up and go over to her out of sheer embarrassment.

One time I was sitting in a coffee shop on Baggot Street. Bridget was walking out of the ladies' toilet looking as if she had just shot up. Una stormed into the coffee shop, ignored my hellos, walked up to Bridget and floored her with a powerful left hook under the jaw. Bridget stayed down while Una threatened her that if she ever robbed a punter off her again she'd cut her heart out and give it to the dogs.

The bouncer did not do any bouncing but wisely sat the episode out until Una had left. His wisdom did not pay off, however, as Bridget gave him a swipe when he tried to help her up.

'My brudders are going to fuckin' mill her,' she said.

'Calm down, Bridget,' I said in as authoritative a voice as possible.

Bridget ignored me. She got up and walked out of the coffee shop with her cute little nose in the air, feigning a sort of dignity. She didn't realize that there were several potato chips stuck to the back of her coat. I hadn't the heart to tell her.

If you met Bridget for the first time, you would be taken in by her raw charm, her super-flat Dublin accent and her mock naïvéte. If you are a man or a mother, your protective instincts would be triggered and you'd fall into a tight trap. Many of Bridget's acquaintances are her victims, often forgiving her after being duped and then suckered by her natural charm. But Bridget is no ordinary street girl addict.

She was a witness to murder. Not very long ago, a young working girl was brutally murdered on the beat. Her bloodied corpse was laced with multiple stab wounds.

As usual the working-girl community and its drug-related fringes became mute. But most streetwise people know who did it, and many know that Bridget was near the spot where the girl died. She was killed as an 'example' because she had ripped off a well-known drug dealer. The police launched a massive inquiry and although they know who did it, there is little they can do for lack of evidence.

I once quizzed Bridget about Sinéad's horrible end.

'Did you know Sinéad?' I asked.

'A bit.'

'Well you certainly knew the people that are sup-posed to have killed her.'

'No way,' she said.

'Bridget, you live around the corner from them, you grew up with them, you bought gear off them for years, you slept with one of them for years.'

'Dey had nuddin to do wid ih!' she protested.

'Well, everyone else thinks so,' I said.

'Well, youse and everyone else is wrong,' said Bridget.

'Ah, c'mon Bridget, don't insult my intelligence.'

Bridget got hold of my arm, pinching it slightly, and walked me away from where we could be overheard. She pushed me gently against a wall and pressed her hand firmly into my chest.

'Now looka Dayuv, the best ting youse can do is stop asking me stupeh questions. I have warrants already and I don't want the shicalonies on me back. I know nuttin' about Sinéad, except that the stupeh gobshite shouldn't have robbed her dealer.'

I moved her hand away from my chest, giving her a doubtful look. I felt like slapping her across the face. I didn't. I turned around to walk away, but she grabbed me by the arm. I shook myself free.

'Dayuv, listen, keep out of dis,' said Bridget.

'Keep away from me,' I said.

As I walked away, I could feel her eyes burning into my back.

Since that conversation she has kept a low profile, not mixing with anyone in particular, and spending little or no time outside the Spar shop. Like all working girls, she used to be seen at the end of the night frantic to find a heroin dealer. That does not seem to be the case anymore. I never see her sick now, and she spends a lot less time walking the beat. I have a theory that she has been given a little 'shut up' money. Either way it is doubtful that the murder of Sinéad Kelly will ever be solved, despite the hard work of the police.

8

STELLA

STELLA IS PROBABLY the nicest working girl I've met. Kind and good-natured, she tries to find good in everybody. She is always smiling and laughing, despite having led a very hard life. She remembers kindnesses and tries to repay them when she can. She is loyal to her friends and has often stuck by me when I was in hot water. I think the world of her. Everyone I know is fond of Stella, but nobody was fond of the appendage that pimped her for years.

Donal was a long-term boyfriend and the father of her young daughter. When she went to work, Donal would stand a short distance from her, waiting for her to get enough money so that he could go and buy heroin. If she was having a bad night, there was no sympathy, just a slap or a mouthful of verbal abuse.

It is hard to believe that in the days of the Celtic Tiger, people still live in hovels. But Stella and Donal did. They shared a tiny one-room flat with another prostitute called Mary. I have been fortunate enough to travel extensively abroad and I've seen extreme poverty in Africa and Asia, but never anything like this. Water, not damp, was seeping down the walls. The smell of rot was everywhere. The carpet was maggoty. The three of them had moved everything over to the side of the room to avoid getting wet. The toilet was unique in the sense that you could sit on it and view the hallway below. I wasn't surprised when Stella and Donal decided to give up the hovel and move into the derelict mental hospital at Grangegorman. This too was open to the elements, but at least the walls were dry and there was a roof over their heads.

What amazed me was how Stella took pride in her appearance. Most homeless street girls end up not caring for themselves as their self-esteem steadily declines, but Stella managed to dress well and keep herself spotless. The cars always slowed down for her.

We used to meet regularly, rarely on the beat, but sometimes for lunch in town when Donal was out of the way. Then one day she disappeared and I got worried. It turned out that she was in custody in Mountjoy for accumulated warrants. I went to visit her. I have never seen her looking so well. She had put on weight, her skin was clear, and there was a glint in her lovely blue eyes. She was delighted to see me and our fifteen minutes went very quickly. She told me she'd had enough of Donal and she just wanted to go home to her mother.

I was invited out to Tallaght to meet her mother. She is a tough, brash woman with a warm heart, a little too fond of the drink. After her mother attempted to marry me off to Stella, it was obvious to me that Stella was not going to last there. A Corporation house full of kids out of control and intoxicated adults was just not for her. We agreed that I would put her up in a bed and breakfast.

Before long she was back on the game and the gear, and with Donal again. I gave up and did not see her for a few weeks until one night, whizzing past Wilton Terrace, I saw Donal slapping her again. She ran off and I caught her. I turned around with the absolute intention of giving Donal a good hiding, but Stella talked me out of it. Again she went back to him and he spent another evening lurking around the beat waiting for her to finish. I couldn't understand why she stayed with him.

Later she disappeared again. No Stella, no Donal. I was worried and started asking around. Nobody seemed to know anything. I phoned the Joy; she was not there. I phoned her mother and she put the phone down on me. Sometime later I received a telephone call from her.

'I'm in love.'

'Who with?'

'James.'

'That northern punter you're always talking about?'

'He's not a punter anymore.'

'Are you sure you're doing the right thing, Stella?' I asked. 'You know that punter relationships rarely work out.'

'I know, Dave, but this guy is really special, he treats me with respect.'

'Stella, I don't want to sound like a bastard, but once they're getting sex you're royalty. Do you get my drift?'

'I just knew you'd say something like that, Dave,' said Stella. 'But you're completely wrong.'

'How am I wrong?'

'We've agreed not to make love for at least six weeks until I feel confident that he is not using me.'

'Well, that's definitely a good thing,' I admitted. 'But just be careful. You've had enough hurt in your life.'

'I'll be alright,' said Stella. 'Sure, I can always talk to my old friend if I'm down, can't I?'

'Of course you can.'

I replaced the receiver feeling at least she had some hope of happiness.

She'd often spoken to me of James. Like a lot of punters, he used to tell her that he loved her and wanted to marry her, but she felt that she meant it. She always talked at length about his ways. James, true to his word, set up house with her in Dundrum, away from all her old haunts. Her heroin intake was dramatically reduced and she spent a lot of time and money trying to get methadone on the black market.

Occasionally, when James headed back up north for a weekend, she would venture out onto the beat for the sake of 'a few spare quid', as she put it.

One night she asked me to pick her up and take her to work. James had gone north for the weekend and she decided she was going to bring punters back to the flat and earn some good money. I told her she couldn't possibly respect James, let alone love him, if she was having sex with punters in his home. She ended up in tears, but I won the argument. A working girl can easily dissociate business sex from personal sex, but they forget that their partners can't, and they take enormous risks when they go to work on the sly.

James and Stella loved each other deeply. She came to me in a state when he asked her to marry him. She felt that she would give him a very hard life because of her drug addiction. But James got involved: Stella became a dealer, and he delivered. Selling drugs only intensified Stella's habit.

One afternoon I decided to confront her with reality. It took more than a quarter of an hour to rouse her at her front door. When she opened up I got a shock. Her hair was knotted and tatty, her speech was slurred, and she was only wearing a pair of panties and a skimpy top. Her legs were a mass of sores and bruises, and her thighs were in bad shape. She barely acknowledged me, turned around and went into the sitting-room. I followed her.

'Stella, where did you get those bruises from?'

'Turn-ons,' she said.

I knew that for every few bruises there would be at least one abscess. There were no abscesses on Stella.

'He's hitting you, isn't he?'

'He's not. They're from banging up. You should know that, you've seen me do it often enough. James would never hit me.'

I stared at her and refused to look away. Stella began to feel uncomfortable.

'Stella, I'm your friend. I'm not going to sit around and let some bloke give you a hiding when he feels like it. No woman deserves that, no matter what the circumstances.'

'He never beat me, Dave, he just gave me the odd dig; and, to be honest, the way I've behaved I deserve a lot worse.'

'No you don't, Stella. James is not some innocent country boy up in the big smoke being roped in by pretty girls. He's my age and he knew what he was letting himself in for.'

'No he didn't.'

'For God's sake, Stella, he was a punter. You were sex. Your nice personality and good looks made you an instant girlfriend for him.'

'But he didn't know about my habit.'

'Stella, not all those bruises are from turn-ons. I can see bruises where there are no veins. I don't see any abscesses.'

'The veins have already collapsed. I just can't mainline any more. Honestly, Dave, he's only given me a few slaps when I've lied to him. Do you think I'd be mad enough to tell you that he was hitting me if it was true? You'd bleeding murder him.'

I put my arms around her again. I knew I was wasting my time.

I didn't speak to her for a while but I wanted to contact her to wish her well and ensure that she kept in touch. I phoned for a few days but got no answer. Finally, I managed to get hold of James's company number and gave him a call.

'We got busted by the drugs squad,' said James.

'Where?'

'At the house.'

'Was Stella done?'

'She was the only one charged, but four of us spent a day in the station.'

'Did she get bail?'

'Yep, and they only found a few bags on her, so I don't think she'll go down.'

'James, the best thing you two can do is get the hell out of Dublin, head back up north and don't come back here for your holidays,' I said.

'Well, we don't have a choice. Some bastard ratted on us to the landlord and we were thrown out,' said James.

'Where are you living now?'

'I'm heading north tonight, and I've put Stella up in a hostel.'

'What's its name? I want to see her.'

The following morning I called around to the hostel near Gardiner Street. Stella was pleased to see me. Despite the trauma she'd been through, she seemed in reasonable form. We sat on the bed and chatted, drinking tea with that horrible powdered milk guesthouses delight in supplying.

'I was ratted on,' said Stella.

'How do you know that.'

'If I said "Christine" or "Claire" to you, would that give you an idea? They both stayed with me at different times last week.' She gazed into my face for a response.

'I'm not sure about Claire, but everyone knows that Chrissy is a rat.'

'It's worse than that,' said Stella, raising her eyebrows. 'I caught Chrissy red-handed robbing my gear money from my hidey-hole. I gave her a few slaps and threw her out. A few days before that, Claire stole all my gear and vanished.'

'Do you know where the drug squad were from?' I asked.

She named a city-centre station.

'How do you know that?'

'I've only spent half a day in a cell there,' said Stella sarcastically.

I wondered that the hell they were doing raiding a house that came under Dundrum drug squad territory. I cupped Stella's chin and looked directly into her eyes.

'What happens when one drug squad raids another drug squad's territory?'

Stella stared at me for a while, then a wave of realization washed over her.

'Christine is well in with the old bill down there.'

'Correct,' I answered, a little triumphantly.

Stella jumped up and threw an overloaded ashtray against the wall. I got hold of her and sat her down again.

'I'm a stupid fucking eejit!' she shouted, clenching her fists and hitting the pillow with her head.

'No you're not,' I said, trying to calm her. 'You're soft like me. She probably came to you saying she'd nowhere to stay and you fell for it. You're just too soft.'

'Wait till you see how fuckin' soft I am after I've given that whore a striping.'

'Look, Stella, the police have got you. The best thing you can do is go north and lie low. Don't react to that bitch,' I said, hoping that by the time she'd settled, her anger would die down.

I haven't seen Stella since, but I spoke to her on the phone. She went up north to be with James and was put on a doctor's list for treatment. She since returned to Dublin for her court hearing. She'll probably escape without a custodial sentence. It is good that at least something came out of the raid: a second chance.

9

PENNY

LIKE MOST OF THE other girls, Penny lost her father when she was young. She still maintains that's when everything went wrong with her life. There is an awful lot wrong with her life. At seventeen, she's a working girl and a heroin addict who has spent time in prison. Her mother drinks and her only brother is in prison for robbery.

When her dad died of a heart attack at the age of forty-six, Penny was thirteen, and it was apparent that her mother couldn't cope. Not long afterwards, Penny got in with a boy nicknamed Devo – by all accounts a genuine love match. Unfortunately part of that love match involved heroin, and Penny was soon completely strung out. When I met her first she was down to her last veins and trying to secure a fix was a frustrating and painful ordeal. Devo had long been locked up in the Joy, and the only way Penny was going to get money for gear was to sell her body. Tall, thin, Latin-looking and very pretty, she soon found the sex business lucrative.

I was introduced to Penny by Karis and asked to take her home to Crumlin. On the way she questioned me about my background and seemed genuinely interested in my education. She told me that was all she wished for, and I assured her that she could get her wish if she wanted it enough. That was the start of our frequent 'lessons'. We discussed everything from religion to local history, and every other night we went over what we had talked about the night before. Penny was intelligent and her life was a tragic waste. But she had a raw ambition to improve herself no matter how difficult the circumstances. I used to bring her to work most nights, and we became good friends.

She talked a lot about her father. They were close, and I felt Penny never truly got over losing him. She sent me a card telling me that I was like a father to her. Rightly or wrongly, I attempted to fill that role. While Devo was in prison, she got mixed up with another boy nicknamed Beano. I was informed from different sources that Beano was a headcase. I contacted her and warned her that if she stayed with him, I'd have nothing more to do with her. I really thought she would ignore me, but she didn't.

One of my favourite pastimes was sitting in the taxi with Penny, putting our seats back and pretending to look towards heaven. We would tell each other tall stories and laugh ourselves sick. We would sit in the car talking for ages, and for a while she would forget that she was strung out and on the game. Our feelings for each other were strong, if platonic. After a while, I detected a lot of friction from Penny regarding Sorcha. I had spent some money on clothes for Sorcha and Penny took this to heart. She could not understand that Sorcha badly needed kitting out, and that I would happily have done the same for her if she ever needed it.

Penny's street bravado used to alarm me; she was always going to beat somebody up and for a time I feared that she would hurt Sorcha, but she didn't. She had always mixed in with boys for whom violence conferred status and a measure of self-esteem. And all the time, there was this normal girl trying to break out and go to parties, school and dates. Instead, she spends her life gathering resources to feed an insatiable heroin habit.

Penny made many valiant attempts to get off heroin and get off the game. At one point she stopped injecting and returned to smoking heroin, a huge watershed to an addict. It gave her the incentive to go for broke, and for

a while she was off the heroin and on a methadone programme. She was now talking about going to school
and sitting for her Junior Certificate. I felt that she was
too enthusiastic and tried to temper her ambitions. I
encouraged her but let her know that if she failed the
first time round it was not the end of the world.

Some time ago, I found Penny staggering across
Mount Street, looking very drunk. As it turned out, she
was not drunk, but had taken a vast number of Valium
tablets. I managed to get her into the taxi and I drove
her home. By this stage, she had fallen into a stupor and
her speech had become incoherent. To make matters
worse, I could not find her house key. As I was walking
her to her front door, she became very aggressive and
punched me several times. Searching her was futile, and
so I walked her back to the taxi and telephoned a friend
who offered to put her up for the night.

Penny seemed to slump into a coma and I became
very alarmed. I drove fast to St Vincent's Hospital. As I
carried her in she came to and decided to attack the
security man. After a bit of a struggle with nurses,
myself and the security man, we managed to put her
into a bed. The doctor on duty assured me after exam-
ining her that she would be all right. I decided to go
home. The next day she telephoned me as if nothing had
happened. I was livid and drove out to her house to confront her. Penny was genuinely sorry and promised that

she would never take tablets again. To my knowledge, she has not done so since.

Lately, Penny has fallen in with another fellow, Teddy, a drug addict, ex-jailbird and occasional con man. Teddy moved into her house and the state of the place deteriorated dramatically, with needles, empty gear bags and general filth all over the place. I ran the risk of being told where to go and mind my own business.

'Penny, I have nothing against Teddy except what he's doing to you,' I said.

'Teddy is good company, he looks after me.'

'Oh yeah,' I responded, the heat rising on the back of my neck. 'He looks after you so well that you have to go out every other night to sell your body in order to get him gear. Then you have to come back to this place and wallow through a pile of rubbish just to get to the toilet which, incidentally, is in an awful state. If he really loved you, he wouldn't have you on the street, this place would be spotless and the two of you would be doing everything to kick your habits and sort out a future.'

Penny looked at me with sorrowful eyes. I could read behind them. If there was no Teddy, she would be lonely. Her brother was locked up and her mother basically didn't give a toss what happened to her. She had nowhere to go. But I couldn't stop what had to come out of my mouth.

'Penny, he's a nice guy but like every addict, he's a user. You suit his predicament. You've given him a place to live, someone to sleep with and someone to give him gear. It can't go on like this. I know you love him, but I'm certain that you're not in love with him.'

'He goes out and robs for me when I can't get anything!' she protested.

'How gallant of him,' I said. 'Listen, Penny, the only reason he robs is that he doesn't want some seedy punter climbing into your knickers. He doesn't do it for you but for himself.'

Her mouth opened to say something, but I forged on.

'Penny, him robbing and you street-walking will lead you nowhere except finally to prison. Whatever his intentions, he's dragged you down and I've had to witness it. I tell you now, your brother is going to go mental when he gets out. If your dad was alive today, there would have been none of these so-called boyfriends and if you'd been strung out then, I guarantee that you would be on some rehabilitation course. You owe it to yourself, love, to at least try and sort your life out.'

She cried a little and I put my arm around her. I never had a daughter, but even in her woeful state, Penny was my daughter then. She needed all the normal love that parents and a brother could give her. Instead, she got affection from a heavily strung-out boyfriend and, on occasion, from a taxi driver. It was a very raw deal. The only hope was the close bond between herself and her brother. He was due out of prison in a few months and I hoped that he would give her what she really needed, family support.

Penny was always buying me presents and worrying when I was down. Some time ago, she bought me a little teddy bear which I keep on my dashboard. We decided to call him Manuel. I look forward to the day when we are sitting in the car together again, our seats back, looking up.

10

TERESA

TERESA IS TWENTY-FOUR years old and smokes heroin, preferring to keep her body free of the marks of drug abuse. She has a Valium habit as well, but her close friend Charlotte has managed to help her keep it under control.

Teresa was born in a small industrial town in the north-east of England to Irish parents. When she was about eight her drunken stepfather climbed into her bed and had oral sex with her. She never found the courage to tell her mother about it as that relationship was catastrophic too. But she remembers lying there, frozen in terror, as her stepfather inflicted himself on her. If this wasn't bad enough, her deranged mother tried to stab her soon afterwards. Both her mother and her stepfather seemed to be permanently drunk, and when her mother told her stepfather 'I tried to kill her', he comforted her, while Teresa was left in her room. Some time later, her mother packed a bag for her, gave her a note, and put her on a bus to the social welfare office in town. One of her most vivid memories as she arrived in the children's home was a poster of Superman which read: 'I too was a foster child.'

Teresa kept running away and soon ended up in a problem children's residential centre. Eventually her mother had a change of heart and demanded her back. The social services refused. Teresa had told them about her sexual abuse ordeals. When this was relayed to her mother, she refused to believe it, saying, 'My daughter is an attention seeker.' Eventually, her mother went to the courts and managed to get custody of her daughter, only to throw her out again two weeks later. Teresa was brought back to another children's home but ran away again, encouraged by her mother. By this time, mother and daughter had moved back to Ireland and into a corporation estate in Inchicore.

The next time her mother threw her out, Teresa went to live on the streets. She was barely eleven years old. She shared a squat with other homeless people in Inchicore. A few weeks later, some men dragged her into a flat and gang-raped her. There were eight of them and she vividly recalls that three managed to have full intercourse with her, while the other five couldn't, which was to her detriment as she got beaten up instead. As a result of this ordeal she became pregnant, but she refused to have an abortion. Her mother took her back and worked on her. Teresa buckled under the severe pressure and went to England to stay with her natural father and arrange an abortion. She views this event with great anguish and looks on her abortion as the loss of a child. While she was recovering, her father presented himself in her bedroom and removed her nightshirt to fondle her breasts. When he had finished abusing his daughter he presented her with twenty pounds. She spoke to her stepsister about this and her sister dismissed the episode as fairly normal. She said her dad was lonely and regularly visited her to fondle her breasts, but never touched her below the belt.

After Teresa recovered from the abortion she returned to Ireland but wouldn't go back to her original home, because her mother was by now a chronic alcoholic and her behaviour was violent and unpredictable. At twelve years old, Teresa was an itinerant child, sometimes sleeping in doorways, sometimes in a squat. By this stage, she had not tried drugs, and if someone had rescued her, she might have had the chance of a normal life. She did get assistance from social welfare in the form of £3 per weekday and £12 at the weekend.

At thirteen she was pregnant again. She was allocated a flat in Rathmines. It was of course impossible to live on under £30 a week, so she tried prostitution. It is not hard to see how a thirteen-year-old girl would understand that if her own father would pay her for sex, other men would do the same. Her first night on the game on Burlington Road netted her £80, and she was delighted. She obtained a new flat on the South Circular Road and let her boyfriend move in.

She and her boyfriend started arguing, mainly because of his drink problem. As a result of this and the fact that she was under age, the social services came with the police to take her two-month-old baby away. Teresa felt it was better for him to be fostered, but those who know her feel that the loss of her child did untold damage.

Teresa began to hate sex and her relationship foundered. She was on her own again, a young girl with no family, her childhood whipped away from her in a cloud of sexual abuse, drunken brawls and unbelievable ineptitude by the authorities.

Her life now revolves around a cycle of heroin, Valium and prostitution. She has had very little contact with her family. She misses her son desperately but has resigned herself to the view that he is better off where he is. Teresa can burst into a hearty laugh at the silliest of jokes. Sometimes she behaves like a naïve little girl unaware of the pitfalls in life. She has been diagnosed with epilepsy, a condition which leaves a girl very vulnerable but more so if she is on the game. In the recent heroin drought, Teresa became very depressed and slashed her wrists. Luckily, Charlotte got to her in time and saved her.

Because of Teresa's gentle and somewhat eccentric nature, other working girls tend either to avoid her or badger her. She can stand up to this but crumbles when the police give her a hard time. She genuinely believes she gives her punters a good service, and cannot understand why such actions are illegal.

In many ways, Teresa is a true child of the street, surviving against brutally unfair odds. As she gets older, things will get harder. Not so long ago, I learned that she had been taken into St James's Hospital, long term. One of her lungs had collapsed, probably due to the toxins taken in from smoking heroin, and she was painfully thin with severe weight-loss. There was talk that she would die. She was in hospital for a long time but has since reappeared, on the beat again around Fitzwilliam Square.

I have heard that Teresa and Charlotte are now 'clean' and are simply out earning money to go to England. I was elated to hear that they had both kicked their habits until I saw Teresa buy what I thought was heroin from a dealer on Fitzwilliam Square. I pulled the taxi over to where she was standing and scared the dealer off. It was a busy night and punters and police cars were everywhere. The dealer jumped on a bike and cycled away furiously.

'Jaysus, you scared the bollocks out of me,' said Teresa. 'I thought you were the Guards. Your man Spanky has done a runner.'

I walked up to her and placed my hands on her shoulders, making sure that by holding her I would have direct eye contact.

'I was told that you and Charlotte were off the gear.'

'I *am* off the gear,' said Teresa defensively, shaking herself free. 'This is charlie.'

'Christ, Teresa, if you're going silly on the coke, you might as well go back to the gear,' I said.

'Ah, Dave, it's only a treat. Anyway, I want to thank you,' she said, stepping closer to me and giving me a quick hug.

'For what?' I asked.

'Well, your man thought you were the police and did a runner.'

'So?'

She looked at me intently. Her sad blue eyes showed the faintest glimmer of joy. Despite a missing tooth, she gave me the sexiest of grins.

'Look!' she said, holding up two tiny bags of cocaine. 'I never paid him!'

'For Pete's sake, Teresa, put them away before we're arrested!' I said.

Teresa gave me a slightly hurt look. She turned around, squatted, plunged her hand between her legs and stood up again.

'What are you doing now?' I asked.

'Piping it,' said Teresa.

'Look,' I said incredulously, 'he'll be back for his money and you'd better have it. Remember what happened to Sinéad.'

'No, he won't,' said Teresa. 'He thinks that your taxi was a police car. He's already on a few charges, so I don't think he'd have the balls to come back here for a while.'

'But what if he finds you somewhere else?' I asked. I thought of Sinéad lying dead.

'I'll just tell him that the cops confiscated the charlie,' said Teresa, smiling at me and looking as if she had just solved a huge world problem.

I decided that it was not a good idea to stick around. I drove off, asking her to phone me. I made sure to drive off in the opposite direction from that taken by the drug dealer.

Just as I rounded the corner onto Fitzwilliam Street, a squad car passed me and I saw it pull up alongside Teresa. I learned later that she had been arrested for loitering and that the police had not found any cocaine on her. She was locked up in a cell in Harcourt Terrace Garda station. They had tried giving her a bad time, but she had the last laugh, if it can be called that. While she was alone in her cell she extracted the coke from her vagina and snorted it. Normally, Teresa would go to pieces if she was arrested, but the cocaine had given her a false confidence.

She demanded methadone and got it, since the gardai didn't know that she was clean. Then she demanded a solicitor, a cleaner cell and some food. The story goes that the police got fed up with her and let her out on Garda bail, telling her that she must appear in court the following morning. As she walked out, she took a small amount of methadone, poured it into a condom and knotted it. Methadone is a sought-after commodity. It was a good night for Teresa; she had got cocaine and methadone, and stood up to the police, all in one evening. It didn't seem like a victory to me, but I had to admit that any joy Teresa felt was worth it.

11

AILEEN

SHE HAS ONE OF THOSE sexy baby voices, and it haunts you long after she's gone. You can't mimic it, but you would recognize it anywhere. I met Aileen through Janey. She hopped into my taxi and started chatting to me non-stop. I thought at first her baby voice was an act, but soon found out that it was the real thing. Aileen was a tall strawberry blonde with a full, curvy figure. Her big green eyes would fix themselves on you and her whole face would become animated with excitement when she was trying to make a point. Heroin addiction and a fondness for cocaine has since altered her naturally pleasant disposition and reduced her to a thin, pale-looking girl. Still, she has no trouble selling her body on the beat down on Burlington Road.

Aileen had a father until six months ago. Her mother disappeared some years back. She is now sharing a flat with her brother, a heroin addict, and Aileen supports his habit when she can. She seems to think that he doesn't know what she does for a living, which is hard to believe since she is out on the streets almost every night.

Her family was from Donegal, but both children were reared in suburban Dublin. She had a deep love for her father, who was very ill for a long time before he died. Her long-time boyfriend was doing time in the Joy. Aileen smuggled some heroin to him and he overdosed. He had been depressed and was facing a six-year prison term, but no one will ever know whether he deliberately took his own life or not. I have seen his picture in Aileen's flat, but she refuses to talk about him.

I remember driving along Waterloo Road when Aileen flagged me down. She was distraught. It took me a long time to find out of what was wrong. Her dad was at death's door and she was heartbroken.

'How bad is he?' I asked, wondering how the hell to comfort a street girl about to lose her dad.

'Only a few hours, I think,' said Aileen, her eyes now very red.

'C'mon, I'll bring you home out of all this shit,' I said.

'No, I'm staying here,' said Aileen. 'I don't want to see him die. I just want to keep business as usual.'

I looked at her and was lost for an answer. This life was 'normal' to her. She would be bent over in some dark alley being screwed while her dad died in a hospital bed. People have different ways of coping with grief.

'You think I'm bad, don't you?' asked Aileen, studying my face.

'No, I don't, love,' I said. 'It's just that I don't like leaving you here when you're so upset.'

'I'll be alright.'

'Are you sure?'

'Yep!'

Aileen sat up and gave me a kiss on the cheek. I held her hand for what seemed a long time, asking someone inside my head to comfort her, to hold her, to save her further pain. I saw her walk up Waterloo Road, her hair tangled and her jeans scraping the wet ground.

A few days later Aileen phoned me to tell me her dad had died. She had gone up to Donegal with her brother for the funeral.

'It's over now,' she said.

'At least he's free from pain.'

'You're right, Dave, free from all the pain I gave him.'

'Aileen, you know that's not what I meant.'

'I know, Dave, but he's gone and I left him nothing to be proud of.'

'Well, now is your opportunity to do something to make him proud.'

I told Aileen to keep in touch, but it was a long time before I heard from her again.

Aileen used to be very friendly with Sorcha. They both had big cocaine habits and used the same taxi driver, Mick the Coke. Every now and then they would fall out, usually over drugs, but something would always bring them back together.

Then Aileen's physical appearance began to deteriorate. She used to deck out in very stylish clothes, but she was reduced to faded jeans and tops that had seen the washing machine too many times. Occasionally, you could say she was really making an effort to look well, but she slipped back into shabbiness all the time.

Her mental state was far worse. Aileen used to have a gentle, caring nature. Those characteristics were still there, but there were times when her cocaine habit manifested itself ambiguously. Sometimes she could be quite paranoid about the most trivial things, like dropping cigarette ash and worrying that she was going to catch fire. Other times, she would come over as if she were invincible, that nothing could shake her confidence. She used to have an attractive walk; now I would often see her strutting arrogantly as if she owned the world.

She started robbing her punters. I met her recently and she was annoyed with herself for not grabbing an opportunity to rob an American punter of $500 he had in his trousers. One day, she will try to steal something off a punter and she will get caught. I dread to think what might happen to her.

Aileen's contacts with the drug world were extensive. In late 1998 addicts were suffering one of the worst droughts in years, due mainly to successful police operations. It was simply very hard to purchase heroin, and when it was available it was sold at grossly inflated prices, or sold at market prices but of very poor quality.

Aileen was one of the few girls who always managed to get her heroin and cocaine somehow. Always on the watch for 'rats', she was cagey about her contacts and wouldn't speak about them. Once she trusted you, though, you were a friend for life and she would do anything to help.

She demonstrated her loyalty some months ago when she was cornered by a ban garda on the beat. Apparently the policewoman had quizzed her about me, suggesting I was drug dealer. Aileen ate the head off her and made it very clear that I was no such thing. She probably made the policewoman suspicious by her strong reaction, but not deliberately. I felt chuffed at the way she stuck up for me.

I met Aileen again recently. She was annoyed that I had 'kidnapped' Sorcha and brought her back to her mother's house in Wicklow. But after a long talk, she saw my point. She had warned me about Sorcha, saying that I should never fall in love with a working girl.

Then, driving back from Fatima Mansions, I saw Aileen sitting on the footpath beside a statue of the Virgin Mary. She looked very ill. I pulled the car over to her, but she was heavily stoned and found it hard to speak.

'Who's looking after you?' I asked.

'Me, as usual,' said Aileen with a weak smile.

'Why didn't you phone me?'

'I lost your number.'

I got out of the car and gave her my number and a hug. She yelped in pain.

'What's wrong?' I asked.

'I've blown my groin,' said Aileen. 'The pain is unbelievable.'

'Is there anything I can do?'

'I'll phone you.'

I haven't heard from Aileen since, but I have heard from others. Her father left her a tidy sum. She's no longer on the beat or in the usual drug haunts. I hope that she and her brother have used the money to get treatment. I suspect that's unlikely.

12

JANEY

JANEY LOST HER DAD when she was sixteen and this seems to have had a profound effect on her. Her association with drugs goes back to her early teens, when her brother James became heavily involved in heroin. Janey was soon strung out, too. Eventually her mother threw her out of their Crumlin house and she had to turn to prostitution to earn a living and support her habit. She lived on the streets, slept in doorways or depended on clients to let her stay the night. Her heroin habit became heavier and soon she was 'using'. After a period of time, her body was laced with track marks, sores, and holes where abscesses had healed. She took the courageous decision to step back to smoking heroin and somehow managed to contain her habit.

Janey likes to work on her own. She finds that when the working girls get together, it 'wrecks her head'. She cannot abide the malicious gossip and back-biting, but she always seems to know the latest piece of street-girl news. She is also an expert at evading the police, moving from one side of the canal to the other, avoiding one Garda station in favour of another. Some of her clients are policemen and it is possible that she gets favours. I know of one occasion when she lifted a policeman's I.D. badge and managed to get a lot of her outstanding warrants cleared for its return. Recently, things have got too hot for her in Baggot Street and she has moved across the river to her old stomping ground, Benburb Street.

It has been suggested by some experts that working girls ultimately hate men. This isn't true of Janey. Her professional sexual encounters may mean nothing to her except revenue, but she has had some long-term relationships. She has a baby girl by one former long-term boyfriend, and it is heartening to see what great happiness it has brought them. Her mother, who didn't talk to her for years, has re-entered her life as a result of the child.

Janey has an ambiguous relationship with her mother, who is keenly aware of her daughter's drug problem. Her mother rejected her father for a woman, and Janey feels this blow led to her father's early death. She loved her dad deeply and resented her mother for rejecting him.

And it was a long time before Janey formed a friendship with her mother's girlfriend.

Loyalties change like the wind among working girls, but Janey's are always well-founded and firm. Sometimes, though, she can be an awful slag. I remember one time I was up in her flat and she was giving me a hard time. She opened the door, calling me 'fatso'.

'Who are you calling fatso, drop-arse?' I responded.

We were soon in the deep end of a slagging match until I was literally floored by Janey. She held me down and because of her immense strength I couldn't get up. She pinned my arms down and made me apologize for my drop-arse remark and admit ten times that I had a big stomach.

I only have to look into Janey's eyes and my heart melts.

She often gets into my taxi for a chat. She tells me stories about her clients, dividing them into likes and dislikes. Her physical stature intimidates some men who may have violent designs, but she's still been attacked several times, which has left psychological if not physical scars. Like most working girls, she carries a weapon to defend herself. The recent murder of a young prostitute frightened her and made her more aware of the dangers she exposes herself to every night. I worry about her safety, especially because she works on her own.

Janey's biggest preoccupation is arranging her life to support her heroin intake. Even when she discovered she was pregnant, she did little to reduce her habit. I often discussed with her the consequences of staying on the drug while pregnant. The prospect of delivering a strung-out baby haunted her, as did the possibility that she could lose the baby to social services. Thankfully, neither happened. Her biggest fear, though, was that the father of the baby was a punter, not her boyfriend. But the little girl looked very like her dad.

As she gets more and more devoted to her child, her desire to lead a normal life increases. She talks about having another child. She keeps her flat spotless and tastefully decorated, like the home of any young family. But every night at about 11, she walks the streets.

There is no doubt that Janey wants to get off heroin and that she really hates what she does for a living. But like many of the more enlightened long-term addicts, she realizes that she might never kick the habit. She still leads a double life in relation to her own family.

Her ex-boyfriend, the father of her child, was no fool; he knew she was on the game with an expensive habit to support. He accepted her work on the condition she didn't have full sex with her punters. If he could have found a different Janey, off the drugs and off the game, he would have done. He knew that the two problems are ultimately inseparable. Even so, she walked out on him.

The two of them just couldn't cope with the heroin taking over her life. Nothing stops him from seeing his daughter, though, least of all Janey.

Recently, Janey walked into a drugs raid. The police gave her a hard time, threatening to take her baby off her and bring it to Temple Street Hospital. They eventually let her go, but have been up to visit at her apartment, looking for information and suggesting that she might be subject to a charge. The visit was official, and the enquiring male police officer made sure he had a female officer to accompany him. Janey would do anything to protect her baby and ex-boyfriend, and the police do not seem to realize that she knows very little and that even if she did, she would not rat on anyone.

Times are hard for her. Her heroin intake has increased and she is having problems finding a safe home for herself and the baby. She has lost a lot of weight, probably from stress as much as her drug habit. But her devotion to her child keeps her going. If the baby were to be taken away, her world would cave in.

13

IMELDA

I FIRST MET IMELDA when she staggered out onto Burlington Road to flag my taxi down. In the process I nearly ran her down. Her mascara was running down her cheeks in the heavy rain. Just as I was about to chew her head off for nearly getting herself killed, she jumped into the car, smiling.

'Marino,' she said. My anger was instantly diffused.

Imelda is big, fierce and strong, but with a beautiful, feminine aura that even the most outwardly good-looking women do not possess. Her sex appeal is in the way she walks, talks and gesticulates. She has huge green eyes and a ringer of a smile that gets to everyone.

Imelda is one of those rare drug addicts who manage to keep a small measure of normality in their lives. She lives in a small terraced house with two beautiful children and her partner. Unlike the other girls, she doesn't work every night, but comes out when she needs money. Nearly all her punters are regulars she has known for some time. Her business is brisk and she can come and go from the red-light district quickly. She is one of the most street-wise working girls I've ever met. She takes heroin, methadone, cocaine and a vast array of tablets, but she exercises amazing self-control.

Her house is immaculate and, despite her large habit, her daughters seem to be normal and balanced. When she goes off to work at night they think she is working at a nightclub. It is lovely to see her put them to bed at night but sad when she closes the door on a comfortable world.

As Imelda and I became closer, I learned that she suffered from a chronic depressive disorder. There were times when I would find her standing in a shop porch with her head hung down. I would go up and attempt to talk to her. She would be perfectly coherent but unable to conduct a proper conversation. The pain expressed on her face would haunt me for days. A few days later she would be herself again – bright, breezy and incisive. Imelda is loyal and can keep secrets, a great rarity among working girls. She is also most perceptive and many of the girls go to her when they have problems.

She commands a high level of respect on the streets from the other girls and even the police.

Her knowledge of the local drug scene is expansive. Imelda can always give expert advice on who sells the best gear and where to get good cocaine, which is not easy in Dublin. She can always get a vein quickly, not just on herself but on others who may be tearing their hair out trying to get a hit. Maybe we get along so well because I also suffer from depression. There was a time where I wanted to get some heroin just to rescue myself from despair. Imelda wisely talked me out of it.

'Are ye tick or wha?'

'Imelda, I can't go on like this.'

'Can't go on? You haven't a fuckin' clue what it's like. You try and bring up anything like that again an' it won't be a spike I'll be stickin' in yer arm, but a boot up yer hole.'

'Well, thanks for your sympathy,' I said.

'You don't need fuckin' sympathy, just a bucket of sense! Haven't I told you before that if yer feeling shite to get in touch with me?'

'Yes, you did,' I responded meekly.

'If you top yerself, I'll fuckin' moorder yeh.'

If I did manage to top myself, Imelda threatened to bring me to life again by injecting an eighth of cocaine into my heart, and when I recovered she would kick the crap out of me. Only two true depressives can get a good laugh out of talking suicide.

True to her street credibility, Imelda does not take kindly to rats, bad dealers, and some of the other girls who have crossed her path in the past. One day I was giving her and another working girl a lift home when a fight started. The other girl came off far worse and by the time Imelda had chased her out of the car she was holding large chunks of her hair. I tried to restrain her, but her immense anger had made her even stronger. Imelda never forgets a hurt or an injury and I'm sure that other girl will come a cropper before too long. But in fairness to Imelda, she will forget about the fight entirely if the other girl makes peace signs.

I remember picking her up in town once when she suddenly leapt out of the car and attacked another working girl she saw walking down the street. I managed to drag her off and prise them apart. It turned out that the other girl had stolen a bag of her heroin and Imelda was paying her back the only way she knew how. A couple of days later they made peace and now Imelda won't hear anything against her. She has a great capacity to forgive.

I would often take Imelda home to her place and stay for a cup of tea. I delighted in her children and became fond of her partner. They managed to keep a normal family home. The romantic relationship between them was long over, but it had been replaced by a close working friendship focused on the well-being of their children.

In many ways, she is an enigma. Most girls with her experience would either be dead, in an institution or in prison. But somehow Imelda seems to have risen above her crippling addictions and kept her persona intact.

On the game, another aspect of Imelda's personality comes to light. I often see her strolling down Burlington Road dressed to kill. She walks with a confident stride, classy sex appeal and sophistication; clean and well-kept, she sees her doctor on a regular basis. Every time I pick her up to take her to work, she is just out of the bath, freshly scrubbed and gleaming. She is renowned for her hair style and wears a series of hairpieces; a natural brunette, she often appears as a stunning blond.

Like many of the other working girls, Imelda has her own well-defined moral code. She would never rob off a punter, but is an expert shoplifter. She would never lie to save her hide and despises anyone even suspected of being a rat. Unusually for working girls I have known, Imelda flatly refuses to discuss intimate details about her clients, let alone disclose their names. Any attempt I have made to enquire into this area has been met with a curt dismissal and sometimes a lecture that I should know better.

Most addicts are self-indulgent and always direct the conversation to the subject of drugs. Imelda is not like that. She would listen with great sympathy to another girl's plight. She has been known to give considerable amounts from her own earnings to other girls who have had a bad night.

Recently, she decided to go onto a methadone programme, but was still taking large quantities of cocaine and pills. I asked her directly about quitting all drugs and for first time got an honest answer. She told me that she could never see herself totally clean. She felt she was too far gone and was cursed.

One early Friday morning I got a call on my mobile.

'What is it, love?' I asked when I heard Imelda crying.

'Pick us up at Abrakebabra and rush.'

The line went dead. Was she hurt, raped, beaten up? I drove fast through the empty streets of Dublin, jumping red lights when I could. If anything happened to Imelda it would break my heart. I had images of Bob hurting her. I was going to kill him. By the time I'd arrived, I had whipped myself into a frenzy of emotion. I saw her beckoning me at the window of the fast-food joint. Her face was contorted.

'What happened?'

'I blew an artery, just below the groin.'

She was crying from the severity of the pain.

'I'll take you to casualty,' I said as I gently put my arm around her waist and lifted her.

'I'm not going into any bleeding hospital. Take me home.'

'Imelda, you have to get that looked at,' I responded with increasing anxiety.

It was no use. Imelda flatly refused to go anywhere except home. I helped her to the taxi, stopping to glare at a group of other drivers who were staring. I could almost smell their disapproval. I got her home and she went to her armchair to rest with her feet up. This time I was not going to argue with her. I telephoned the emergency doctor and he called quickly. You never really know how a doctor is going to react to a drug addict. They can be basically sympathetic or completely insensitive to a suffering addict's plight. Many doctors today have broken their Hippocratic oath by being selective about who they look after. But this doctor was very gentle and caring, doing everything he could to make Imelda comfortable.

She had done serious damage to herself. She'd correctly entered her vein with the right size needle, but had slipped off a toilet seat. The impact of falling had pushed the needle through the vein, through a major artery and through one of her main nerves, rendering her left leg powerless. When feeling started to return, it came back with a vengeance in the form of extreme pain. The doctor prescribed powerful pain-killers, ordered her to rest and told her that she could be out of action for months.

Not Imelda. She was back on the beat in two weeks, worrying about the welfare of her children. At first I refused to take her to work but realized that it made no difference; she would only take the bus.

14

AOIFE

IT WAS A WET, murky night. The type of night when everyone stays indoors. I was driving around Benburb Street looking for Janey. A young girl stepped out in front of me, and I braked. The taxi came to a halt about a foot away from her. She placed her two hands on my bonnet and smiled at me through the windscreen. I sat there, surprised. She walked around to my car.

'Do you want to do business?'

'No thanks,' I answered. 'But can I take you anywhere?'

She walked around the car, using the bonnet for assistance and got in beside me.

'Take me home.'

'Where's home?'

'Anywhere at all,' she said.

Accepting that my passenger seemed to be stoned out of her face, I thought it best to get her out of the Benburb Street area as quickly as possible. Even on wet nights, there was always the odd individual ready to take advantage.

'So, where are we going?' I asked.

'Nowhere really, I just want to get away from that psycho.'

'What psycho?' I asked, alarm bells ringing in my head.

'My fella. He caught me getting into a punter's car. He's going to murder me.'

I drove on up to the lights on Parkgate Street.

'What's your name?'

'Aoife.'

'Aoife, where do you live?'

'Ballyer, but I can't go back now, my fella could be there.'

Just as she finished speaking, a man jumped into the back and grabbed Aoife from behind.

'Ya fuckin' scabby little whore,' he roared.

Aoife tried to scream, but the pressure on her neck from this madman made her choke. I had to do something quick.

I jumped out and opened the back door. A fist landed in my stomach. I fell backwards and landed in a sitting-down position on the pavement. I lost my breath. The man was pulling Aoife out of the car. He kept on punching and slapping her. I pulled the belt off my trousers. I leapt on the man's back and whipped my belt around his neck. He started choking, and released his grip on Aoife. I pulled away and placed my knee hard into his lower back. I managed to get him on the pavement and hold him down.

'Get back in the taxi,' I yelled to Aoife.

She jumped into the driver's seat and started the engine. With the crashing of gears she accelerated off, breaking the lights in the direction of the Phoenix Park. The guy I was holding down started a spluttery laugh. I pulled his head up by the hair.

'Where's she gone?' I asked.

He spat at me right in the face. I saw red. I punched him just under his nose. He groaned and passed out. I got the belt and tied his hands and legs together while he was still lying on the pavement. I dragged him along to the railings that border the Croppy Acre on Benburb Street. I had to leave him there and find my taxi, knowing full well that he would free himself in a few minutes and come after me.

I started walking in the direction of the Phoenix Park. A few minutes later, a set of headlights came towards me. My taxi pulled up and the front passenger door swung open.

'Get in,' said Aoife, keeping the taxi in gear for a quick getaway.

Aoife drove rapidly through the Park. We pulled over in a dark corner near the Ashtown Gate. I was still panting and the sweat was pouring off me.

'Are you alright?' asked Aoife.

I didn't answer right away. I just stared at this young and pretty working girl. Ten minutes ago, I was picking up a passenger. In a short period I'd rescued her from strangulation and ended up getting attacked myself. Then the girl I tried to save drove off in my taxi.

'Why did you steal my taxi?' I asked.

'I didn't fuckin' steal it. I was trying to get away from yer man.'

'Yeh, and you left me behind,' I said, feeling a little hurt.

'Didn't I come back for ye?'

I sat back in my seat and started to wonder how I get myself into these situations. Aoife put her hand down her bra and pulled out what looked like a lump of earth.

'What's that?' I asked.

'Marla.'

'Marla? That's the Irish for plasticine.'

'It's also the nickname for hash.'

Within minutes Aoife had expertly rolled a joint. I didn't want any and told her so. Nor did I want her smoking it in my taxi, but I had no energy to protest anymore, so I let her. I put my seat back and nodded off. I woke up to a rocking sensation. I looked around and it was daylight. Why was the car rocking? I turned my head and let out a scream. A cross-eyed girl with buck teeth had pressed her face against my window. It was Aoife. She gave me a fright and was now laughing her head off.

I thought to myself that two can play this game. I started the taxi and drove off, watching her chase it in my rear-view mirror. I drove around for about ten minutes and then went back to pick her up. I was all prepared to carry on the joking, but got a surprise.

'You were going to leave me!' said Aoife, her face all flushed from crying.

'Aoife, I was only joking.'

'No, you were going to leave me, you bastard.'

It didn't take long to realize that I had upset her badly. I felt so guilty that I checked her into a guesthouse for a few nights to give her time to find a more permanent address.

We lost touch, and I often wondered if she was safe and away from her lunatic boyfriend.

Later I heard on the grapevine that Aoife had done very well. She had completed a detox course and was now working on a farm outside Galway city. Her boyfriend had been locked up for a long time for grievous bodily harm.

It is now well over a year since I encountered Aoife, but I have heard that she is off all drugs, has met a man who loves her, and is happy. It is so heart-warming to know that at least one or two girls – against unbelievable odds – do make it.

15

GINA

I WAS DRIVING DOWN Herbert Place looking forward to a nice hot bath and a long sleep when I eyed a
shapely redhead flagging me down.

'Can you take me up to Ballybough, love?'

'Hop in,' I said with a smile, wondering who I was
speaking to.

'You're Dave, Sorcha's fella, aren't you?'

'I was, not now.'

'Well, listen, love, you're better off. All those girls end
up breaking your heart.'

'Have you a fella yourself?'

'No, I have a girlfriend,' she said, giving me a smile.

'You must find it hard doing business out there if
you're gay,' I said, puzzled.

'I certainly do, but not for the reasons you think.'

'What do you mean?'

'I only wear my ghee when I go to work. I'm Barry,' she said, her smile now turning into a laugh.

'Well, you fooled me.'

'I fool a lot of people, love,' she said, 'that's the business we're in.'

'What happens when a bloke finds out you're a bloke?' I asked.

'He never gets a chance,' she said. 'As soon as he drops the hand too far, I do a runner.'

'It must be scary,' I said.

'Believe me, love, it's not half as scary as not having enough money for gear.'

'You said your name was Barry,' I asked, 'but do you have a girl's name?'

'I'm Gina until I take my ghee off, Barry at all other times.'

'Which do you prefer, Gina or Barry?' I asked, intrigued.

'It all depends on the situation, love. Many of the girls out there don't even know that I cross the tracks all the time, and I love that,' she said.

'Love what?'

'It might sound daft, but I get a huge buzz when people don't suspect I have a dick,' said Gina. 'It's like I was always a girl. And when I get out of here, I want to get home and fuck my girlfriend's brains out,' she said, laughing.

'Does she know that you cross the tracks?'

'Oh yeah, she helps me buy all my clothes. We have an understanding.'

Gina and I developed our own understanding. I liked her and she liked me. At least I liked Gina. I met Barry a few times and was not so sure. Barry came across as a little too butch, the male side being pushed in your face. My uncertainty was confirmed when I found out that Barry had given his girlfriend a few thumps.

Whether it was true or not that Barry was a girl-basher, Gina was the bravest woman I have ever met. To 'come out' from the cold, to smack life in the face, to contend with the gibes, the remarks and outright hostility, takes courage. Gina is tough, she's decent and I have never known her to take a knock lying down. Thrown on the slagheap when she was a little boy, she spent much of her childhood in care.

I knew of her through my friend Janey, who was fascinated with her disposition. Gina had come on the game when she developed a heroin habit. Unlike many of the other girls, she set herself high standards and refused to let herself slide. Her deportment is excellent, she's spotlessly clean; Gina could pass herself off as a career woman or a lady about town anytime.

Her girlfriend Sally seemed to take the whole thing in her stride. She, too, was a working girl, well used to all sorts. Sally would tell me about the times Gina would 'regress' into a violent version of Barry. Luckily, Sally is no walkover and was well able to handle Barry when he became violent.

When I first bumped into Barry, I was given a great welcome, but was not quite sure who I was talking to. It took a while to register and I stumbled over my words, uncertain how to address him.

Some time ago, Gina and Karis flagged me down on St Stephen's Green. They wanted a lift to Richmond Street where they were sharing a flat. On the way, they asked me to stop at a shop. I was waiting around the corner when I heard a commotion. I jumped out of the taxi, ran around the corner and saw that Gina had jumped on the counter, leapt onto the shop attendant and was in the process of beating the crap out of him. I stood there frozen.

Karis managed to drag Gina off and they both jumped into the taxi as I was driving off. The shop attentant was lying on the floor clutching his testicles, writhing in agony. The damage to the shop was considerable; there were chocolate bars and sweets all over the place mixed in with mashed cakes and bottles of pop. When they got into the taxi I angrily demanded an explanation. It turned out that the shop attendant had raped Gina some months ago, taken her money and had got away with it. She swore that she had not planned to go looking for him, but that she recognized him as soon as she walked into the shop and had snapped.

Every time Gina goes on the beat she is at risk. She sells herself as a woman, giving hand relief and oral sex. I have often seen her with a black eye or bruises all over from clients who have discovered her secret. A few punters do not seem to mind that she is transsexual, and still others were attracted to her because of it. Sometimes, clients who know she is a man demand anal sex and she obliges, knowing that if she doesn't, she could be beaten up or worse. She'd say, 'Up the gicker, five times quicker!' On occasions I could tell that she was in a lot of pain. She would take a few days off to recuperate, and then turn up again right as rain.

Lately, Gina has not been seen on the beat at all. Many of the girls have asked me about her whereabouts. Gina was completely accepted as one of the them, without reservation, and when she vanished, they missed her. I found out that she had moved her work down to the quays and was selling herself strictly as 'gay' rather than as a working girl.

I bumped into her in town and she looked remarkably well and happy. She had got herself off heroin and was not taking any form of drugs. She was in fighting spirits. Her relationship with her girlfriend had finally come to an end, but there was a new man in her life who was looking after her. It became apparent that all she ever wanted was to be accepted as a normal woman, and her new boyfriend has contributed to that objective. I was thrilled that she had kicked her heroin habit into the gutter.

16

BLINKY

HER REAL NAME is Dolores. She didn't ask for the nickname 'Blinky' and nobody is quite sure how she got it, but the name stuck as did all the other problems that came her way. Blinky is a child of the slums, Ballymun, product of a dysfunctional family, dead father, absent mother and a brother who is both a heroin addict and an alcoholic. She has a sister in London she cares for, but there seems to be little contact.

I first met her in a restaurant near Benburb Street while breakfasting with Janey one dreary Tuesday morning at about 3 a.m. She walked in, greeted Janey, sat down beside me and, as can be expected from much of our youth today, completely ignored me. I didn't ignore her. She could not have been more than fourteen.

Underneath the scruffy clothes there was an exceptionally pretty girl.

'What the hell is a young one like yourself doing out
here in the morning?' I asked.

Blinky went very red. She was embarrassed. Janey
sensed the situation and decided to introduce me.

'Don't worry, Blinks, Dave is a friend,' said Janey.
'He probably thinks you only look about twelve years
old.'

'I'm seventeen,' said Blinky, 'and what has it got to
do with you anyway, old man?'

'Nothing really,' I said, smarting. 'I was just wondering.'

'Well, I'm not on the game if that's what you think,'
said Blinky, her face still flushed.

'No, I don't think that,' I said. 'I suppose you're up
here looking for gear.'

'I'm not on gear,' said Blinky.

'And I've got two heads,' I said.

There was an awkward silence. I suddenly felt a stabbing pain in my ankle. Janey gave me a filthy look, but
I pushed on. I turned around and fixed a gentle and sincere gaze into her eyes.

'Look, Blinky, or whatever your name is, if you're
not strung out on something, how do you explain that
horrible mess on your wrist?'

Blinky grabbed her wrist and pulled her sleeve down

over her abscess. Her face seemed to go a redder shade of red.

'So, I'm strung out, so what?' she said. 'What's it got to do with you?'

'And you're not seventeen,' I answered.

'She is, Dave,' said Janey. 'I know her mother, she's from the Mun and strung out to bits.'

'Yeh, like half the kids in Ballymun,' said Blinky.

'And she's not on the game,' said Janey.

'So what are you doing here?' I asked.

'I'm looking for gear,' said Blinky.

Janey raised her eyes to heaven and wagged her finger at me, indicating I was pushing it a bit.

'Blinky, the Mun is awash with gear, you only have to walk up to anyone on the road. If they don't have anything, they'll point out someone that does,' I said.

'Who the fuck are you, my father?' remarked Blinky, her face red.

'How about an Irish breakfast?' I asked, trying to diffuse the situation.

'Yeh,' she said.

Cigarettes were flashed all around and the atmosphere became a little more relaxed. The prospect of a big breakfast seemed to cheer her up. Her bright red face toned down to its natural colours. For a while the conversation became a piss-taking contest between Janey and myself. Blinky loved it.

'Dave, your stomach is getting fatter,' said Janey with a smirk.

'And your arse is getting huge,' I said.

'You can't even see my arse,' said Janey.

'It's just as well,' I said. 'It would blot out young Blinky here completely.'

'You'll never have the privilege of viewing my bum.'

'It wouldn't be a privilege, it would be torture,' I retorted, 'and anyway the smell would probably kill me.'

A sodden chip landed on my head. I returned the fire. Then Blinky joined in by throwing the remains of a rasher on my lap. I was made to apologize for my remarks and admit that my stomach was the size of Phoenix Park. The ice was broken.

Once again I asked Blinky what she was doing down on Parkgate Street.

'I'm at large,' she said.

'How come?' I asked.

'I was sentenced to two years for robbing and I did a runner as I was taken out of the court.'

'So why aren't you hiding somewhere?' I asked.

Blinky looked at Janey, Janey looked at me and I looked at Blinky.

'You've nowhere to go, have you?' I asked.

Blinky nodded her head. Her face started to go red again and she burst into tears. I put my arm around her and let her cry.

'Blinks!' I said.

'Wha?' she asked, her face buried deep into my sleeve.

'Do you always make pig noises when you cry?' I asked.

She pushed me away, laughing. Janey joined in by suggesting that at least she didn't act like a pig like I did. I excused myself and went to sit at another table. I wanted to phone Mick the Coke. The girls looked a little puzzled.

'Mick, I need a favour. I want you to put someone up for a week so that she can lie low and get her head together.'

'I can't, Dave, my grandma is up from Galway for a month,' said Mick.

'Mick, your grandparents have been dead for years. You told me that last week when you were stoned out of your face,' I said, lying, but knowing he was probably lying too.

'Did I?'

'Yes, you did.'

'Look, I can't let any brazzer from the street stay with me,' said Mick.

'Fuck the neighbours, you should be worrying what will I think if you don't put her up,' I said.

'Dave, I know I owe you some favours, but you can't expect me to put a total stranger up for a week,' protested Mick.

'Mick, I'm not calling in any favours, she's just a kid and she needs a roof over her until she gets sorted out,' I said.

'Why can't she stay with you?' asked Mick.

'You know my reputation about the girls,' I said.

'The whoremaster,' said Mick with a laugh.

'Well, can you imagine what it would be like if anyone discovered that I had a young one staying with me?' I asked. 'I'd be labelled as some kind of pervy paedophile.'

'They could say the same about me,' said Mick.

'True, Mick, but only me and a few others know where you live,' I said.

'Okay, Dave, but only for a week,' said Mick. 'She's out after a week.'

'Thanks Mick. I'll be up to you in an hour or so.'

'Bye.'

'Mick!'

'What?'

'If you lay a finger on her, I'll have your balls cut off,' I added.

'For fuck's sake, Dave, what the hell do you think I am?' asked Mick.

'I mean it, Mick, she's not to be touched by anyone, she's only a kid.'

'Dave, you know me, I like big tits, plenty of charlie and a bird with money,' said Mick with a measure of sincerity.

Mick had never let me down. He had a strict regime in his house. Everything and everyone had to be spotlessly clean. Everyone had to muck in with the chores, throwing in a few quid if they had it. If they had no money, they would be looked after anyway. The only drawback was the loud rock music Mick played habitually as he gyrated in ecstasy on one of his many cocaine binges. Blinky would be all right for a little while.

The drive took over an hour. Mick lived in an old farmhouse without a farm, but with a few half-crazed hens that staggered around the yard clucking very loudly. I'd swear that he had them on cocaine.

Nobody ever discussed how Mick made his living, nobody dared to. But he probably sold cocaine direct to street dealers. Anyone staying with him could not buy off him and 'did their own shit'. It was a golden rule. Despite his own addiction, I knew that Blinky would be safe. Mick would try and talk some sense into her when he was not on coke, and otherwise she'd be left to her own devices.

Blinky stayed for four days. Mick bought her a load of new clothes, probably financed her habit and handed her two hundred pounds sterling when she decided to go.

'Did she give herself up at the Joy?' I asked.

'Did she, bollocks,' said Mick. 'I put her on the ferry. I got in touch with her sister in London. She's going to look after her.'

I just hoped her sister would look after her. How could her mother not care for her? The answer was probably heroin.

Occasionally, Janey and I would talk about Blinky, wondering whether she would make something of herself in England. I got an answer in an envelope on one Friday morning. The letter had been addressed to Mick's farm and he had mailed it on to me. It was labelled, 'For Dave, Mr Fat Stomach,' and read:

> Dear Dave,
> Just a short line to let you know that everything is okay over here. The Brits aren't all that bad, except they don't know how to chill out. I am going out with this culchie called Liam. He's great crack. I'm off the gear and on the foy! What do you think of that? I get scared shitless every time I see a cop or a cop car. I'm working in this restaurant for £200 a week! Me and Liam are getting a flat next week. He works in a record shop. Thanks for looking after me. I'm sneaking home this Christmas. I'll get in touch. Love you to bitz!
> Blinky xxxx.

The letter was finished with an imprint of a kiss made out of very bright lipstick.

17

CLAIRE

I WAS DRIVING Karis home one night and a girl called Claire got in the taxi with her. Like most of the other girls, she was very pretty, overdressed and looking a little unhealthy, probably from drug abuse. As soon as they drove off they started bickering over some punter. I was not in the mood for this. I set the meter and loudly interrupted to inquire where they were going, hoping that my angry tone might change things. Karis was heading home to her flat in Phibsboro, but as yet Claire was too intent on arguing with her to give me an answer.

'Where the hell are you going, Claire?' I roared.

'Someone has had a bad day,' said Claire.

'Listen, Claire, I just want to know where you're heading so I can pick up the next fare, alright?'

THE BEAT: LIFE ON THE STREETS

'Take me to the Malahide Road after you've dropped off her ladyship,' answered Claire.

I pulled over outside Karis's flat. The girls had stopped fighting but there was still a tense silence. Karis gave me a kiss on the cheek, threw a five pound note into my lap and left, slamming the door. Our usual nightly chat was scuppered by the presence of Claire. I drove off expecting a silent ride.

'Fucking little toe rag,' I heard from the back. I chose to ignore the remark rather than launch into a defence of Karis.

It wasn't long before we were driving through the outskirts of Dublin. The last buildings had disappeared and Claire directed me up to what looked like an abandoned cottage. She asked me to shine the headlights at a pile of rotting timber. She jumped out of the taxi and vanished behind the timber for a few seconds, returning with a small bundle wrapped in plastic.

I got out of the car. 'What have you got there?'

'When was the last time you took coke?'

'Never.'

Claire opened up the small parcel and revealed an ounce or so of cocaine. She pinched a little bit of it and snorted it up her nose. Her pupils immediately enlarged and she looked almost radiant.

'Are you alright?' I asked, wondering if she was still aware I was beside her.

'This is fucking rocket fuel!' she quipped, ignoring my question. She took another pinch and stuffed it up her nose.

'In the car,' she ordered. I complied, not knowing what I was getting myself into, but feeling good. Claire leaned over my seat and pulled the recliner lever. I shot back suddenly and found her trying to straddle me.

'Claire, what the fuck are you doing?' I asked.

'Trust me,' she said.

In an instant she was kissing me and removing her shirt. Soon I was inside her, wondering how I had gone from picking up a relative stranger to having her body impaled on my penis. Before I could reach the point of no return, she stopped, bent over, put her hand on my mouth tightly and started kissing my eyes. I breathed through my nose, wondering if she got sexual pleasure from trying to smother me. Within seconds I felt a bitter taste at the back of my throat and realized that I had snorted some cocaine. I pushed her off. She sat up and looked at me intently.

'You fucking bitch!' I screamed.

There was no response for a moment and then she ordered me to sit back. I was waiting for her to say something, but my intense anger seemed to dissipate. My erection was beginning to hurt. She scooped up some more coke, snorted most of it and rubbed the remainder around the tip of my penis. I felt a pleasant numbness. I remember thinking 'Is that it? Is that what this insipid white powdery stuff is all about? How disappointing!' But within a minute or so my heart started to beat faster. I froze.

Claire leaned over me again and started to caress me. All hell seemed to break loose and I felt as if a high-speed train had entered the top of my head and was charging through me. My toes were tingling. The sensation was mind-boggling. As all this was happening, Claire impaled herself on me again.

My feelings of sexual intensity were magnified. I had never experienced such raw pleasure, but no matter how hard I tried I could not come. We seemed to go on all night. Eventually, things came to a head and it was over. Time meant nothing to me. I knew I had been having sex for a long time, but when we finished it seemed like it was only for a few minutes. I felt exhausted and not a little sore.

Claire offered me a paper hankie to wipe myself. I yelped when I found blood. I was panicking, but somehow she assured me that everything was all right. Apparently the cocaine had not been 'chopped' finely enough and the tooing and froing had caused abrasions. She seemed to know about this and I had no choice but to trust her. I discovered that my nose was bleeding as well and I felt like I had been run over by a truck. Lying there on the driver's seat, I realized I had just taken a highly dangerous and seriously illegal drug with a working girl. I turned around and looked at her.

She smiled back matter-of-factly, as if what had passed between us was a casual encounter, the sort of thing that a taxi driver does every day. I had difficulty in making my mouth move to formulate words, but I was determined to communicate.

'Did I just have sex with you?' I asked.

'No, not really, it was me that did all the work. I just fucked your brains out,' she answered.

'Did you give me some cocaine?' I asked, wanting her to feel at least some of the guilt.

'Yes I did, and you took it.'

'I feel like I've been hit by a steamroller. A couple of hours ago I was driving two working girls home, a few hours later I've just had amazing sex with you and my first cocaine experience,' I said, almost protesting, but not quite sure whether I felt incredulity, anger or delight.

'Yeh, the sex was okay for me, too, bring me home,' said Claire.

'Have you got any of that stuff left?' I inquired.

'About £800 worth.'

'Surely you're not going to use all that!'

'No, I'm going to sell it.'

'But you're on the game!'

'Not any more.'

'Where did you get it?' I asked apprehensively.

'I robbed it off my boyfriend,' she said.

'Oh fuck!'

I felt a chill go down my spine. Her fella was probably huge and when he found out, he'd probably stick me with a long knife. I was scared shitless.

Through the corner of my eye, I felt Claire studying my face.

'Don't worry, love. By the time he finds it's gone, he'll be eating out of my hand.'

'What do you mean?'

'I'll head home and shag him stupid. He thinks I've been working all night. You're my alibi.'

'What are you going to do with all that cocaine?'

'Sell it.'

'No, I mean what are you going to do with it now?' I realized that I was committing a serious crime by letting her carry it in my taxi.

'This is what I am going to do with it,' said Claire as she pulled her knickers down and stuffed the bag of cocaine up her vagina.

We drove on through north Dublin until we reached a prestigious apartment complex in Clontarf. During the course of the journey I saw Claire tear her cigarette packet apart as if she was looking for something. I pulled up outside the apartment foyer.

'See this building?' asked Claire. 'Practically every resident indulges in a bit of charlie every now and then.

This is a golden opportunity for me. It will get me off the game.'

'Do you live here?' I asked.

'Maybe I do and maybe I don't,' she answered. 'I'm not going to tell you in case you're a rat. But here's my phone number. Maybe we'll do it again sometime.'

She stuffed a piece of cigarette paper in my top pocket. I put my hand up to retrieve it but she stopped me.

'Don't look at it now, but when you do, open it very, very carefully. There's a little surprise for you.'

She kneeled over and gently grabbed my pony tail. I put my head back on the headrest as she gave me a very gentle, lingering kiss. She walked out of the taxi towards the foyer deliberately pouting her bottom at me. After she had gone, I just sat there for a while trying to sort out what had happened to me. I placed my hand in my pocket and pulled out the cigarette foil. It contained her telephone number and about two grams of cocaine. I decided to give it back to her so I phoned her, hoping she would come back out and take it. I got her voice mail instead.

'Hi, I'm in the shower at the moment, so please leave your name and number and I'll get back to you.'

I left my number and a message imploring her to get back to me quickly and take this stuff off my hands. I never saw Claire again. I learned later that she was caught selling heroin inside a certain well-known night-club in collusion with the bouncers at the door. All were charged, but Claire decided not to stay for the hearing. She absconded to England.

I didn't use the cocaine. I had better use for it. Bob was giving me a hard time and I needed to get him off my back. I needed to teach him that I could give as good as I got. I arranged for a certain individual to get into his taxi as a paying passenger. The young lady sat in the back seat and deftly taped the cocaine under the concealed portion of the central armrest. She got out at the bottom of Grafton Street and disappeared into the crowd, making sure to give Bob a handsome tip and a sexy wink before she left. A couple of hours later I phoned Bob.

'Hello?'

'Hello Bob, this is your old arch-enemy,' I said.

'I don't want to speak to you,' he said.

'Fine!' I said. 'But let me tell you a little story and then hopefully we'll leave each other for ever.'

'Go on.'

'Under your rear armrest you will find a couple of grams of cocaine. It was placed there about a week ago by someone who would dearly love to hang you. It can be done again and again. Also your family would love to hear what their darling Bobby does at night, pimping young girls and selling drugs.'

'I'm going to destroy you,' said Bob.

'No you're not, Bob,' I said. 'You're going to take care of Amanda and stay away from me forever.'

I switched off my mobile and let out a very deep sigh. It had been a long day. Since that telephone conversation, Bob has kept a low profile. The girls tell me that he won't let anyone in his taxi and is always searching it. I started searching mine a long time ago.

18

DYMPHNA

I WAS BRINGING an old friend home in my taxi, telling him about the book I was writing on working girls. Terry was intrigued. I wanted to get some answers out of him because he was a policeman, and although he had nothing to do with vice or drugs, he might point me in the right direction. I didn't get any information about the legal side of things, but I did get to know a working girl through him. Her name was Dymphna. Terry had no compunction in telling me that he had done business with Dymphna over the years.

'How did you get to know her?' I asked.

'Same as you met Seema, really,' he responded. 'I was in my local and I just got talking to her. She was gorgeous and I fancied the arse off her.'

'Did you know at the time that she was a working girl?'

'I had an idea. I knew right away that she was strung out on gear. When I met her the first time, her pupils were so pinned they were like two black stones in the snow.'

We drove on for a while. I was trying to picture what Dymphna was like. Probably just another working girl with problems, a habit, trying to find somewhere to live while avoiding the police.

'Jaysus, Terry, you must have had some conflict in your head over Dymphna,' I said.

'What do you mean?' he asked.

'Did you not think you were doing anything wrong doing business with a working girl, and you being on the force?'

Terry didn't answer right away. He raised his eyebrow and stroked his nose, choosing the right words. He was like that. Terry rarely reacted quickly to any question, but would always respond after some thought.

'At first, I just wanted sex and because I hadn't been successful with women, I was willing to take the risk and do business with her,' said Terry. 'But after a while, as I got to know her, I started to feel for her.'

'How long have you known her?' I asked.

'About five years now.'

'Five years? And she's never ratted on you?'

Terry gave me a dirty look. He sat forward, deliberately fixing a stare on me. His usually passive expression became clouded with emotion.

'Let me tell you something, Dave. Dymphna is no rat. There were many times where I could have used her and she could have used me. You know me well enough to know that I would never take advantage of a person in a weak position.'

'Terry, you're a cop,' I said.

'Dave, I am a cop, but not all cops are the same,' he answered. 'Just because you've seen some of them at their worst doesn't mean that they're all like that. Like I said, there were many times where I could have used Dymphna, but I didn't. In fact, if I did anything wrong, I helped her when she was in trouble.'

'Like what?' I asked.

'Like never mind, it's none of your business.'

'Can I meet her?' I asked pleadingly.

'No, no fucking way,' said Terry.

'Terry, if your answer is no, then your answer is no. But at least hear me out, okay?'

Terry sat there silent. He lifted his eyes and let out a long sigh. He fixed his gaze on me.

'She is sick, very sick,' he said.

'Like sick, as in not having any gear?'

'No, ironically, she's off the gear, but she's dying, dying slowly,' he said sadly.

'The virus?'

Terry nodded. An image of Seema shot into my mind. It was almost a sadistic image, she was smiling at me knowingly. Soon Terry would go through what I had gone through. Nobody can really comfort you when you lose the one woman you love.

'Terry, did you ever tell her about Seema and me?' I asked.

'I did, and she felt sorry for you. I remember her saying years ago that a man should never get involved with a working girl, it always leads to great pain.'

'She is only too right,' I said.

'Better to love and lose rather than not have loved at all is a load of shit,' he said bitterly.

'I don't know. Losing Seema broke my heart, but if I had the chance to be with her again, nothing would stop me.'

'She nearly destroyed you,' said Terry.

'Yes, I know that.'

Terry placed his hand on my shoulder and shook it gently. I was going to cry. A grown man was pouring his heart out to a policeman. Policeman? Policeman my arse. Terry was just my friend as he had always been. The guy that pulled a works out of my arm when I tried to top myself.

I had injected four bags of heroin, taken five Valium Two tablets and laid on my sheepskin rug with the full intention of dying. I'd had enough, I just wanted to smell Seema's scent again. I just wanted to go. I stood up and inserted the needle into a huge vein on my forearm. I remember thinking that four bags would be enough. My parents already considered me an addict when I wasn't. At least they would think I had overdosed and not topped myself. I started to push the plunger down. A massive wave of sleepiness came over me immediately and then there was nothing. I'd deliberately given Terry a key to my flat and arranged to meet him at my place the following afternoon. I'd given him the job of finding me. I reckoned that being a policeman, he'd know what to do. I left a note instructing him to tell my parents about my accidental overdose. What a bastard I'd been to my friend.

'Wake up, you fucking cunt!' were the first words I heard. 'Wake up!'

A shower of cold water roused me and then I felt excruciating pain. My forearm was twice its normal size. Next minute I saw a bright light and a guy in a green shirt looking down at me. I was in an ambulance. I was still awake, but I couldn't feel or see anything. Was this death? Then it happened. I could pick up my lover's scent. Seema was with me. I tried to see her, but I couldn't. I wanted to ask her why she died on me but I knew she was still angry with me and had just come to see if I was all right.

I woke up again about twelve hours later to a lecture on drug abuse from some musty-looking, middle-aged doctor who was probably used to addicts overdosing all the time. I needed to go home, and I did.

Terry had saved my life. I wanted to thank him and at other times I wanted to shout at him for disturbing me. He would not speak to me for months.

Now he was refusing to let me meet Dymphna, but I knew him well enough to know that he was going to talk to her about me.

Eventually he relented. I was to visit Dymphna in hospital. She was very weak and Terry made me promise that I wouldn't try to pressurize her. I would visit her on the following Tuesday, when she was due to have completed a course of treatment that would help her live a bit longer.

I went to the shop outside my flat and bought a bunch of flowers for Dymphna. As I walked out, my mobile rang. It was Terry.

'Dave, don't go and see her.'

'Why? What is it?'

'She died this morning, about eight o'clock.'

'Jaysus, Terry, I'm so sorry.'

Terry and I belonged to the same club now. I had stood in the same spot for ages, when my friend Vera came up to me.

'She's dead and gone,' I said to her.

'Who is?' asked Vera.

'Seema,' I said.

Vera came up to me and held my hand. I dropped the flowers on the ground. We both knelt down at the same time. She picked them up.

'Seema is gone a long time now,' said Vera gently.

'I know, but she has a friend now. Terry had a lover called Dymphna, she died this morning.'

I started walking back to my flat. I wanted to go home and lie on my sheepskin rug. I needed to be with Terry. He needed me.

'What about these flowers?' shouted Vera.

I didn't answer.